INVESTING IN EVERY CHILD

An Economic Study of the Costs and Benefits of Eliminating Child Labour

International Programme on the Elimination of Child Labour (IPEC)

INVESTING IN EVERY CHILD
An Economic Study of the Costs and Benefits
of Eliminating Child Labour

International Labour Office, Geneva
December 2003

ISBN 92-2-115419-X

First published 2004

Second impression 2004

Photocomposed in Switzerland   WEI
Printed in Switzerland   SRO

FOREWORD

One in every six children aged 5 to 17 worldwide is exploited by child labour in its different forms, according to estimates made by the ILO in 2002. Many of these children are forced to risk their health and their lives and mortgage their future as productive adults.

More information has raised awareness of the scale of the problem and given new urgency to developing and financing policies and programmes to remove children from work situations. More knowledge has also provoked new questions about the cost of removing children from work, providing them with education and ensuring them a decent childhood. At the same time, policymakers are also enquiring to what extent the effective abolition of child labour will pay off for national development and poverty reduction, and how children and their families stand to gain.

This report is based on a wide range of data and technical assumptions about the quantifiable elements of the costs and benefits of ending child labour. While it has to be noted that some important benefits of eliminating child labour such as enhanced possibilities for personal development can hardly be measured in monetary terms, our calculations clearly led us to the conclusion that the elimination of child labour is a high-yielding global investment. With an affordable amount of financial resources, enormous benefits would be generated in all regions of the world. In the light of this finding, we can assert with even more conviction than ever before that the elimination of child labour deserves to be pursued with utmost determination.

The investments necessary to end the scourge of child labour can be made, and they must be made. We owe it to our children to ensure that they can fully develop their talents and strengths, which are the key to the future of their families and societies. We must strive for children to enjoy their childhood, playing, learning and preparing for a decent working life as adults and parents. It is our responsibility to ensure that this is the last generation to be exploited as child labourers.

Frans Röselaers
Director
International Programme on the
Elimination of Child Labour – IPEC

The study was developed and coordinated by Frank Hagemann and Peter Matz. The lead technical advisor was Peter Dorman, who wrote the final report with the assistance of Ana Lúcia Kassouf, Peter Matz, and Sevinc Rende. Important statistical contributions were made by Farhad Mehran. Country-specific data was collected by Ruperto P. Alonzo (Philippines), Kamal Banskota (Nepal), Abdoulaye Diagne (Senegal), Ana Lúcia Kassouf (Brazil), Abdul Razzaq Kemal (Pakistan), Tetyana Kyrian (Ukraine), Germano Mwabu (Kenya), Joseph Semboja (Tanzania), and their teams. Useful comments were provided by colleagues from the ILO, UNICEF, the World Bank, the UNESCO Institute for Statistics, UCW, WHO, and the US Department of Labor.

Funding for this project was provided by the United States Department of Labor.

TABLE OF CONTENTS

Tables

Figures

Boxes

LIST OF ABBREVIATIONS

CBA	Cost-benefit analysis
DALY	Disability-adjusted life year
FFE	Food for Education
FTE	Full-time equivalent
GNI	Gross National Income
HIV/AIDS	Human Immunodeficiency Virus/Acquired Immunodeficiency Syndrome
ILO	International Labour Organization
IPEC	International Programme on the Elimination of Child Labour
KILM	Key Indicators of the Labour Market
LABORSTA	International Labour Office database on labour statistics operated by the ILO Bureau of Statistics
LSMS	Living Standards Measurement Survey
NAR	Net attendance rate
OECD	Organisation for Economic Co-operation and Development
PETI	*Programa de Erradicação do Trabalho Infantil*
PNAD	*Pesquisa Nacional por Amostra de Domicílios*
PPP	Purchasing power parity
PROGRESA	*Programa de Educación, Salud y Alimentación*
PTR	Pupil/teacher ratio
SIMPOC	Statistical Information and Monitoring Programme on Child Labour
UCW	Understanding Children's Work project (Joint ILO/World Bank/UNICEF project)
UNAIDS	Joint United Nations Programme on HIV/AIDS
UNDP	United Nations Development Programme
UNESCO	United Nations Educational, Scientific and Cultural Organization
UNICEF	United Nations Children's Fund
UNHCR	United Nations High Commissioner for Refugees
WDI	World Development Indicators
WHO	World Health Organization
YLL	Years of life lost due to premature mortality
YLD	Years lost due to disability

EXECUTIVE SUMMARY

FINDINGS AND IMPLICATIONS

The goal of eliminating child labour is embodied in ILO conventions, national legislation and the objectives of workers' and employers' and other civil society organizations around the world. But what resources would be required to achieve this goal? What would be the economic consequences, and how would they be distributed across different sectors of the global community?

IPEC has conducted the first integrated study of the economic costs and benefits of eliminating child labour throughout the developing and transitional world. A general programme of action was developed which was hypothetically applied in all countries, and estimations were made of the cost of each element in this programme as well as the projected economic gains from eliminating deleterious child labour and replacing it with education. The study does not tell us *whether* to eliminate child labour – these commitments are already in place – but it sheds light on the financial burden this may entail and the economic impacts we can expect as a result. Equally, it does not offer specific policy prescriptions, since the action programme it models is generic, whereas actual policies must be tailored to specific country conditions – but it provides information that may assist those who formulate policies or campaign for their acceptance.

The programme had these components:

a) Education supply: an expansion of school capacity and an upgrading of school quality, in conformity with ILO Convention No.138, which envisions education as the principal activity for children up to the age of 14. The study estimated both the capital (building construction) and recurrent costs of making this education available to all children not currently attending, while making allowances for changes in the child population. It also considered the cost of reducing class sizes and supplying sufficient materials in instances where current practice does not meet international quality guidelines. The goals set forward were

1

universal primary education by 2015 and universal lower secondary education by 2020. It is important to note that much of this commitment is not unique to our proposed programme; achieving universal primary education is one of the Millennium Development Goals embraced by the world community. In this context we regard child labour elimination as building on already-existing objectives. While we calculate its total cost in this study, it should be borne in mind that the incremental cost of our programme, its addition to costs already entailed by other commitments, is far less.

b)   Income transfers: the institution of income transfer programmes in each country to defray the cost to households of transferring children from work to school. These programmes would target all families with school-age children now living in poverty, providing benefits according to a formula taking into account the average value of children's work, the number of children per household and the degree of the household's poverty.

c)   Non-school interventions: a programme of interventions aiming at the urgent elimination of the worst forms of child labour, in conformity with ILO Convention No. 182. These programmes would remove and, if necessary, rehabilitate children in the unconditional worst forms, such as bonded labour and prostitution, as well as those engaged in hazardous work. Interventions would also target socially excluded children, including refugees and those from lower castes, who may require particular attention. More broadly, we can envision these interventions addressing the cultural factors that often play a crucial role in

Table 1.1. Cost and benefit items

Costs	
Education supply	Costs of building new schools, training and hiring new teachers, supplying additional educational materials
Transfer implementation	Cost of administering the income transfer programme
Interventions	Cost of achieving the urgent elimination of the worst forms of child labour and addressing the needs of special populations
Opportunity cost	Cost borne by households due to the value of child labour foregone

Benefits	
Education	Benefit of improved productivity and earning capacity associated with greater education
Health	Benefit of reduced illnesses and injuries due to the elimination of the worst forms of child labour

reproducing and legitimating child labour, complementing the economic factors addressed by the rest of the programme. Such cultural concerns often have important gender dimensions; while these may be crucial to the planning and implementation of interventions, for the purposes of this study we assume that gender considerations do not have a bearing on programme costs.

These three make up the costs of eliminating child labour, along with the opportunity cost of this labour itself – that is, the economic benefits that would be lost if children were removed from a portion of their productive activities.

Details concerning the calculation of these items will be discussed in this report. For now it should be noted that, as is the usual practice in studies of this sort, the transfer of income itself (from taxpayers to programme beneficiaries) is not regarded as an economic cost, since no "real" resources are allocated in conjunction with the money. Nevertheless, the cost of administering the programme is included, since it absorbs the time and effort of programme officials who might be put to other tasks.

There are also two principal benefits, the added productive capacity a future generation of workers would enjoy due to their increased education, and the economic gains anticipated from improved health due to the elimination of the worst forms of child labour. Of course, there are many other benefits of eliminating child labour, such as enhanced opportunities for personal development and social inclusion, that are resistant to economic quantification. Therefore, this report makes no attempt to account for them.

In order to quantify these costs and benefits, we drew on country data at three levels of detail. Research teams gathered information in eight countries, Brazil, Senegal, Kenya, Tanzania, Ukraine, Pakistan, Nepal and the Philippines; these provided our most complete cases. A second tier consisted of approximately two dozen additional countries for whom household surveys, primarily conducted by IPEC and the World Bank, have been implemented during the past decade. While not complete, these provided a high level of detail for most cost and benefit factors. (These countries are listed in Appendix 2.) For the remaining countries we used publicly available demographic, economic and education data as the basis for extrapolating from those with more complete information. This report presents findings at the global and regional levels, but it also uses our country studies to illustrate some of the issues involved in measurement, and it includes condensed versions of three country reports as illustrative annexes. (The full-length version of these reports will be published separately by IPEC.)

The methodology used in this study takes into consideration alternative estimations at every stage. Thus, there is not one result but a range of possible results, depending on what assumptions are employed. Nevertheless, we have produced a baseline estimate, resting on what we regard as the most plausible, typically mid-range assumptions (see Chapter 2). The results are summarized in Table 1.2.

Table 1.2. Total economic costs and benefits of eliminating child labour over the entire period (2000 to 2020), in $billion, PPP (Percentage of aggregate annual gross national income in parentheses)

Region	Transitional countries	Asia	Latin America	Sub-Saharan Africa	North Africa and Middle East	Global
Total costs	25.6	458.8	76.6	139.5	59.7	760.3
Education supply	8.5	299.1	38.7	107.4	39.6	493.4
Transfer implementation	0.7	6.3	1.2	1.5	1.1	10.7
Interventions	0.4	2.4	5.8	0.6	0.2	9.4
Opportunity cost	16.0	151.0	30.9	30.1	18.8	246.8
Total benefits	149.8	3 321.3	407.2	723.9	504.1	5 106.3
Education	145.8	3 307.2	403.4	721.8	500.2	5 078.4
Health	4.0	14.0	3.8	2.1	3.9	28.0
Net economic benefits	**124.2 (5.1 %)**	**2 862.4 (27.0%)**	**330.6 (9.3%)**	**584.4 (54.0%)**	**444.4 (23.2%)**	**4 346.1 (22.2%)**
Transfer payments	13.1	125.8	23.5	29.1	22.1	213.6
Net financial benefits	**111.1 (4.6%)**	**2 736.6 (25.9%)**	**307.1 (8.7%)**	**555.4 (51.3%)**	**422.3 (22.0%)**	**4 132.5 (21.1%)**

The cost and benefit items are those listed in Table 1.1, with "transfer implementation" referring to the administrative portion of the income transfer programme. By net economic benefits, we mean the difference between total economic costs and total economic benefits. Net financial benefits deduct from this the financial cost to the public sector of the income transfers themselves. The figures are reported by regional grouping and globally, in billions of dollars and as percentages of total income in year 2000. These are discounted present values: they condense the entire stream of costs and benefits over the twenty years of the programme (and further years of education benefits as former children continue to work as adults) into a single number, reducing today's equivalent of future amounts at the rate of 5% per year.

The single most import result is that the elimination of child labour and its replacement by universal education is estimated to yield enormous economic benefits – in addition, of course, to the social and intrinsic benefits that make this issue so salient. Globally, benefits exceed costs by a ratio of 6.7 to 1. This is equivalent, given the time distribution of costs and benefits, to an internal rate of return of 43.8%. These figures, it should be noted, suggest a degree of precision that is not warranted in light of the very large uncertainties in measurement that surround most aspects of this study. As the body of the report makes clear, our tabulations could well be above or below these amounts. Nevertheless, the gap between benefits and costs is so

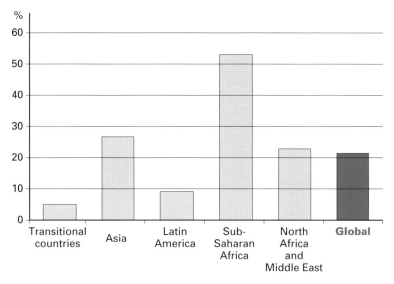

Figure 1.1. Net economic benefits as a percentage
of annual Gross National Income

great that it is sure to withstand reasonable adjustments that might be made to its methodology. All regions experience very large net gains, although some benefit more than others. The same results are displayed graphically in Figure 1.1.

By demonstrating that the benefits of expanded education are well above their costs, this study concurs with research conducted by the World Bank (e.g. Psacharopoulos and Patrinos, 2002) and other institutions that there are significantly positive rates of return from investments in this sector.

A second approach is to consider the economic flows that transpire over the twenty-year duration of the hypothetical programme, followed by the next twenty years of benefits. Figure 1.2 shows the pattern at the global level; regional patterns are similar.

In this figure, undiscounted net annual flows are tracked across time. For the first eight years they trend downward (more negative); then they reverse direction, becoming positive in year 2016. This reveals the economic character of the child labour elimination programme as a generational investment, a sustained commitment to our children in order to reap the benefits when they reach adulthood. For approximately one and a half decades during which the programme is first implemented, its economic burden will exceed its returns. After this the net flows turn positive, dramatically so after 2020, since past this point there are no further costs, only the benefits derived from improved education and health. Hence, taken as

Figure 1.2. Undiscounted annual net economic benefits (costs), in $billion, PPP

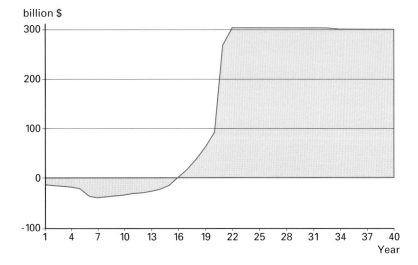

Figure 1.3. Public sector costs of eliminating child labour, in $billion PPP

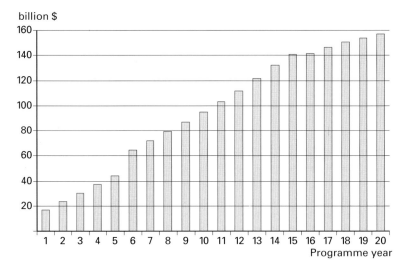

a whole, these delayed benefits more than recoup the costs, even allowing for the effects of discounting (which Figure 1.2 does not). It should be noted that the information in Figure 1.2 does not include the amount of income transfers, since these do not represent a real deduction from the output of society. Incorporation of transfer payments delays the year at

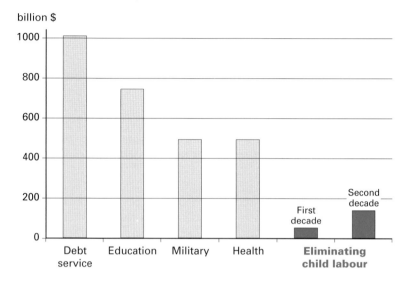

Figure 1.4. Average annual cost of eliminating child labour compared to other annual costs, in $billion PPP

which benefits overtake costs, but it does not fundamentally alter the overall pattern of results.

From a practical standpoint, the burden on the public sector in particular is important to consider. Resources must be mobilized to finance education, the transfer programme and the targeted interventions that make these benefits possible. Figure 1.3 tracks these programme costs over their 20-year duration. It includes the income transfers but excludes opportunity costs borne by households. It also deducts 20% of the benefits that accrue in each year, under the assumption that the public sector would capture about a fifth of these through higher revenues. Costs rise continuously over this period, but less steeply after universal primary attendance is achieved in 2015. Costs end altogether after 2020, as we have seen, so, if we extended this chart beyond that year we would see only the revenue gains associated with the economic benefits (about $60 billion per year).

What would it mean to the world community to make an investment of this magnitude? One way to answer this question is to compare the costs observed in Figure 1.3. with other categories of expenditures. In Figure 1.4. we contrast the average annual cost of eliminating child labour during each of the programme's two decades with four other expenditures on the part of developing economies in the year 2000.

The average annual amount during the first decade pales in comparison with the burdens currently borne to finance debt service or the military; it is even small relative to existing social expenditures. The corresponding average during the second decade is larger, but still manageable in light of the other items, particularly if it follows a period of sustained economic growth.

Putting together these two analyses – net economic benefits and public sector costs – what conclusions can be drawn? Figures 1.2. and 1.3. demonstrate that a protracted period, approximately fifteen years, of net costs is followed by an even longer period of still larger net benefits. Indeed, the costs are complete after 20 years, but the benefits continue for more than 40 years past that point. The critical question is how to finance an investment of this magnitude and duration. We believe that, in light of the existing funds that are potentially available, this is primarily a political rather than economic question. The child labour elimination programme represents a noticeable but not exorbitant increase in current social expenditures (averaging about 11% during the second decade). It should again be stressed in this context that universal primary and lower secondary education, goals which command widespread support already, make up the bulk of our economic costs and benefits. Where we go further is to place them in the context of eliminating child labour, particularly in its worst forms. Thus, the incremental cost of this commitment should be regarded as far less than the total reported here. We therefore hope that some version of this child labour elimination programme can be placed on the table in discussions over debt relief and development assistance.

METHODOLOGY

In the remainder of this summary we will present secondary results and consider the extent to which our findings might be modified on account of the uncertainties surrounding measurement and the assumptions required to perform the necessary calculations.

Chapter 3: Who are the child workers?

Our approach to measuring the extent of child labour is grounded in the two principal ILO conventions governing this question. Convention No. 138 prohibits all economic activity by children beneath the age of 12 and permits light work only for 12 and 13 year-olds in developing countries and 13 and 14 year-olds in the developed world. It calls for universal compulsory education through the age of 14 in developing countries and 15 in the rest. Convention No. 182 prohibits and targets for urgent elimination the worst forms of child labour for all children below the age of 18. Since our study considers only developing and transitional countries, we identified all economically active children below the age of 12, all children ages 12 to 14 working more than 14 hours per week, and all children below age 18 in the worst forms of child labour as "child labourers". We used the same data and similar methods to estimate the 5 to 14 age group as were employed in the recent IPEC report, *Every Child Counts* (ILO, 2002), involving an extrapolation from 28 countries with reliable survey data to the rest of the world. The result was a global enumeration of just over 182 million such children, 18.5% of all children between these ages. (Due to apparent differences in survey methodology, the observations did not prove amenable to extrapolation via regression, so we applied the unweighted regional average of the ratio of working to all children aged 5 to 14 to countries without surveys.) We did not attempt an extrapolation of older children in the worst forms, however; instead, we simply added up the numbers for the countries available to us. This resulted in a total of 10.8 million children in hazardous occupations and between 8 and 20 million in "unconditional" worst forms, such as trafficking, bonded labour and prostitution. Many of these children are under 15 and have therefore already been counted in our estimate of total child labour.

Chapter 4: The cost of increasing the quality and quantity of education.

We used the existing costs of education as a basis for calculating the additional cost of achieving universal attendance, with the following exceptions. First, we checked to see if the pupil-teacher ratio was less than 40; if not, we budgeted the extra funds to achieve this level. Second, we considered whether non-personnel expenses, such as supplies and textbooks, made up 15% of all recurrent costs; if not, we budgeted the difference. We also made adjustments for shortages in the teacher-training capacity of tertiary education, for the role of direct household contributions and for special circumstances like HIV/AIDS in the hardest-hit countries. Based on these calculations for our eight study countries, we extrapolated to the rest of the world, creating low, medium and high estimates.

Net attendance rates (NAR) at primary and lower secondary levels were derived from household surveys, which typically yield lower figures than the enrolment rates reported by education ministries. Globally, the average NAR for primary education was 76.2% and 48.9% for lower secondary. We proposed to close the primary gap in three five-year "waves" beginning in 2000, and the lower secondary gap in three waves beginning in 2005.

Our baseline global cost for achieving 100% NAR at both levels was $493 billion. Our lowest estimate of potential education cost per student resulted in a reduction to $438 billion, while our highest estimate yielded $606 billion. This last figure represents a significant increase, but hardly sufficient to alter the overall results in light of the large surplus we find in Table 1.2.

Chapter 5: The direct household costs of eliminating child labour.

Households in our programme face one major cost and enjoy one major benefit. They lose the economic value of their children's labour as it is progressively eliminated over a 20-year period. But, if they are poor, they stand to benefit from an income transfer programme that is phased in over the same duration. (To the extent that the transfers are not financed by funds diverted from other uses, of course, non-poor household may pay more in taxes.) This chapter estimates each of these and compares them.

Attaching an economic value to the labour of children is a crucial aspect of this study. Perhaps no concern about the desirability of eliminating child labour is more widespread than the notion that households, particularly those in poverty, cannot afford to lose the contribution currently made by their children. Unfortunately, there is little systematic evidence regarding the value of child labour, and the information available to our country teams was not always sufficient. In the end, we chose to assume that a child worker's contribution is 20% of an adult's. This is reflected in our baseline estimates, although raising this fraction to 25% (almost certainly an upper limit) would raise the total cost of eliminating child labour by approximately $60 billion, a minor adjustment in the context of Table 1.2.

The income transfer is a more ambitious version of programmes that have already been implemented, such as Brazil's *Bolsa Escola*. It uses a formula that transfers 60-80% of the average value of child labour per school-age child attending school to poor households irrespective of whether this child is a past or current worker. (The exact percentage depends on the degree of poverty and the number of school-age children per household.) To estimate the total amount of funding such a programme would require, we used our estimates of the value of child labour and extrapolated from survey data on the extent and depth of poverty, as well as the number of school-age children per poor household. Evidence is provided in this chapter that the cost of the transfer programme is not very sensitive to plausible changes in the formula used to calculate it or the estimated value of child labour itself.

Comparing the lost value of child labour and the added income due to transfers, we find that the first exceeds the second by a relatively small margin – $247 to $214 billion. However, these amounts pertain to different populations. Some poor households receive benefits without curtailing child labour because their children were not working previously, and other households curtail child labour without receiving benefits because they are not poor. Thus the moderate aggregate shortfall of the household sector reflects the size of the second group relative to the first.

Chapter 6: Public sector costs of eliminating child labour

There are two principal costs facing the public sector, apart from those having to do with expanding the availability and quality of education. The first is the cost of administering the income transfer programme; the second is the cost of interventions targeting children in the worst forms of child labour and those whose work or lack of schooling is tied to social exclusion. Our primary objective in this second set of activities is the complete elimination of these worst forms by 2010.

We assume that the administrative cost of the transfer programme will amount to 5% of the sum transferred to poor households. This is an arbitrary amount, although not implausible. (*Bolsa Escola* and other existing programmes provide little guidance, since they include other functions in addition to income transfer.) As Table 1.2 indicates, however, the amounts are very small in relation to most other costs and benefits; a doubling of administrative expenses would have virtually no effect on the conclusions of this study.

We calculated intervention costs based on tabulations of the number of children requiring such intervention and the unit costs of past efforts in this field. To achieve the first of these, we added up the number of children identified as working in hazardous conditions or highly excessive hours (more that 43 per week), those in the unconditional worst forms of child labour, those who were included among the refugee populations tabulated by UNHCR, and those whose caste identification in Nepal would suggest their social exclusion. Due to the highly country-specific nature of most of these numbers, we did not attempt to extrapolate them. Thus, our totals significantly undercount the number of children who might be targeted for intervention. On the other hand, we assumed that *every* such child would be targeted, which overstates the cost since many children would be removed from such work due to other aspects of the action programme, and spillover effects would make it likely that interventions would change the circumstances of children who were not their specific targets. Combining these two, it is likely that our underestimate of the number of children to be served is moderate rather than extreme.

Unit costs (costs per child removed from work or rehabilitated) were derived from a study of IPEC projects in 18 countries. They ranged from a low of $139 in North Africa and the Middle East to over $1,600 in Latin America. (A high percentage of Latin American programmes have targeted prostitution, which entails large costs to rehabilitate children.) We applied these averages to the number of children either socially excluded or in the worst forms and arrived at the totals in the row labelled "Interventions" in Table 1.2. This is the smallest of all the cost items. Indeed, even if it were multiplied tenfold it would have relatively little effect on the overall structure of the results.

Chapter 7: The benefits of education

The principal economic benefit from the elimination of child labour would be the enhanced productive capacity stemming from universal education through age 14. This is difficult to dispute, yet it is also difficult to quantify. Ultimately, the economic value of expanded education will depend on other changes taking place within a country over the same period: the effectiveness and stability of its institutions, the creation of new enterprises organized to take advantage of higher levels of human capital, and economic policies to stimulate growth and development, among others. We are not in a position to forecast these factors. Instead, we have relied on recent evidence of the relationship between education and earnings at the individual level, which are predicated on the existing set of institutions and policies.

Estimates of the value of education constructed in this way have been conducted in many countries around the world. We took an average value – that each extra year of schooling results in an additional 11% of future earnings per year – and applied it to all countries. To translate this into amounts of money, we multiplied it by the average unskilled wage prevailing in each country. We also assumed that individuals would begin work at age 15 and retire at age 55. In some respects this is a conservative approach, since it assumes that unskilled wages will not rise over time (except as a result of increased education), that individuals will work for only 40 years, and that education benefits only its direct recipients, and not the rest of society through indirect channels. On the other hand, we may be overestimating the effect of education, since its value might be less for those who do not enter paid employment, might be reduced as it becomes more widespread ("credential inflation"), or might be overestimated in the earnings studies we relied on.

Any monetary value attached to education can be approximate at best. We regard our baseline estimate as plausible. Nevertheless, it is interesting to consider how the results of the study would change if it turned out that education were much less valuable. One way to do this is to lower the percentage effect of years of schooling on earnings. If it were 5% rather than 11% – a reduction of more than half – the global benefit would fall from just over $5 trillion to about $2.3 trillion. This would reduce but not eliminate the large disparity between costs and benefits in our study; it would still exceed $1.6 trillion, yielding an internal rate of return just under 23%.

Chapter 8: Health benefits

ILO Convention No. 182 urges us to give priority to the elimination of the worst forms of child labour. This entails costs, as we have seen in our review of programme interventions. Most of the benefits are humanitarian, yet it is likely that tangible economic gains will accrue from the resulting improvements in child health. It is important to stress that the attempt we have made to quantify these benefits does not signify that we view health as having *only* an economic value. Safeguarding the health of children is vital in many ways; the economic benefit is just one of them and may well be one of the less important. Nevertheless, since this is a study of the economic costs and benefits of eliminating child labour, we are required to estimate the value of improved health in some manner.

Our approach is based on a comparison of potential health gains from eliminating hazardous child labour to those of eliminating certain other health risks that have already been studied for their impact on economic growth. To do this, we need a common system of measurement for the extent of these risks. We adopt the World Health Organization's (WHO) DALY – disability adjusted life year – for this purpose. DALYs express each specific type of health impairment as a fraction of a year of life lost, based on the degree of function lost by the individual. Using this index makes it possible to add up a wide variety of illnesses and injuries and arrive at a single summary number. We selected four high-profile studies of the economic effects of ill health, one on occupational safety and health in the United States and three on malaria in Sub-Saharan Africa. By converting the health risks to DALYs (using data from WHO's *Global Burden of Disease*), we were able to express the results of these studies in the form of percentage of national income lost per DALY.

At this point, the chief difficulty we encountered is the absence of systematic data on the health consequences of hazardous child labour. A special study was therefore commissioned on the health benefits of eliminating child labour (Fassa, 2003). Despite a large quantity of information on the risks faced by specific groups of children, the only nationally representative survey proved to be one conducted in the United States, providing injury incidence rates for children according to major industrial classification. These were converted to DALYs and applied to a set of 18 countries for which we had survey data on the industry composition of child labour. From these we extrapolated to the rest of the world.

The baseline result for health benefits in Table 1.2 reflects this methodology, utilizing an intermediate relationship between DALYs and per capita national income from one of the malaria studies. Two of the malaria studies give a DALY-income relationship approximately one order of magnitude lower, while the occupational safety and health study generates a relationship approximately one order of magnitude higher. Thus, health benefits could well be a tenth of the baseline amount, or ten times that amount.

We believe on intuitive grounds that the baseline relationship is reasonable, since it indicates that for each year of life lost prematurely the society will bear a cost of somewhat less than 40% of its average per capita income. The other major uncertainty stems from the use of United States data as the source for the work-risk relationship in developing and transitional countries. We believe this is probably an underestimate, both because work is likely to be more dangerous in less developed countries, and also because the US data included injuries but not illnesses. Overall, there is a potential for the true economic benefit to be gained from eliminating hazardous child labour to be several times the amount we have estimated.

Chapter 9: Implications of the study for policy and future research

Policy issues have already been addressed in the first section of this summary. From a methodological standpoint, in the course of pursuing the first global study of the economic aspects of child labour and its elimination, we have made more visible key gaps in the available information. A serious commitment to ending child labour will require much more reliable estimates of costs in particular, in order to implement and finance programmes at the national and regional levels. Further research is indicated in such areas as the earnings and productivity of child workers, the evolution of child labour indicators over time within individual countries, the appropriate indicators of educational quality, the accessibility and cost of lower secondary education and the health outcomes associated with the worst forms of child labour. In all of these areas we were forced to make strong assumptions due to lack of hard data. Real, and not hypothetical, policy calls for real data.

METHODOLOGY AND PRINCIPAL RESULTS

2

The ILO perspective is that child labour is not only, nor perhaps even primarily, an economic problem. The justifications for ILO Convention No. 138 (minimum age of work) and No. 182 (worst forms of child labour) are largely ethical and social in nature, although the economic consequences of child labour are also taken into account. By the same token, these conventions do not anticipate that countries should wait until economic development "solves" child labour, if indeed this could ever be expected. Rather, they call for immediate action by all countries at all levels of development.

Notwithstanding these commitments, the ILO has a stake in the ongoing debate about the economic aspects of child labour in general and its worst forms. Those who formulate policy or allocate resources in this field ought to have a rough sense of the economic consequences of different policies. They should know not only the overall economic costs and benefits, but also their distribution across countries and sectors of society. This will help them make realistic judgments regarding the feasibility of child labour elimination programmes, and identify financial bottlenecks that may prevent potential gains from being realized. It is one thing to turn to economics for fully-packaged answers to child labour questions – something we do not do here – and another to provide information about economic aspects to a broader decision-making process.

DEBATES SURROUNDING THE ECONOMIC ASPECTS OF CHILD LABOUR

Much of the debate over child labour in the developed countries since the mid-nineteenth century has centred on economics. Very generally, we can identify three questions:

1) Is child labour really a problem at all? If the economic value contributed by working children exceeds the costs of this activity, should it not be permitted to continue? Some economists are inclined to assume that, if children or their parents choose child labour over its alternatives, it must be the case that the net economic value (benefits minus costs) is positive. A different way of putting this is to ask, if we implement programmes that successfully reduce the prevalence of child labour, will we be making households even worse off than they were previously?

2) If child labour is a problem, is it solved "automatically" in the course of economic development? Is the best course in less developed countries to put preventive activities on hold and wait for economic growth to produce the right conditions for future action?

3) If child labour is a problem that demands immediate attention, are there economic factors ("market failures") that call for correction? If so, what are they?

These questions are inspired by economic theory, which give pride of place to the role of individual choice within the constraints imposed by resources and technology. The tendency within economics is to view undesirable conditions as problems to be solved only if they can be shown to be related to market failures – the task for which conventional economics is designed. From a wider perspective, these questions do not by themselves resolve all the issues that need to be addressed, but they are still worth exploring. Thus, even though, in conformity with ILO conventions, we are committed to eliminating child labour, we would still want to know if households expect to lose more income from the withdrawal of this portion of their labour than they would gain from the beneficial consequences. Similarly, if economic development is related to a reduced incidence of child labour, this would play a role in evaluating tradeoffs between economic and other objectives.

In recent years, much of the economic debate has revolved around the interpretation of the historical record in the developed countries. There is little dispute that these countries have undergone extensive economic development during the past one or two centuries, while also reducing the extent and severity of child labour. The lessons to be drawn from this experience are in dispute, however. It may be that development, by increasing household incomes and the return to education, played the principal role in reduced exploitation of children. It may also be the case, however, that social reform, through legal and political channels, coupled with investments in education, played a larger role, and that the reduction in child labour was itself an explanatory factor in subsequent economic growth.[1] This is not the place to assess the weight of these two arguments, but it is clear that the historical debate is highly relevant to the current situation of developing countries. One contribution of the present study is that it offers evidence regarding the *potential* for immediate action against child labour to spur economic development along the lines of the social-reform approach.

In the course of this investigation, we will also be in a position to shed light on the situation at the household level. Rather than simply assuming that children or parents are accurately weighing economic variables, we will provide empirical estimates of the costs and benefits they face. This information can then be combined with other social or cultural factors – which our study does not consider – to investigate household decision-making criteria.

As for the third question, we are not directly testing for the presence of market failures; nevertheless, the issue is central to our approach. One possible explanation for child labour whose costs exceed its benefits is the failure of credit markets: parents are unable to borrow against the future earnings of their children in order to finance their withdrawal from work and placement in education.[2] While such a situation is undoubtedly common, this study does not pursue credit market reform as a strategy, for two reasons. First, the insufficiency of credit markets to finance investments in human capital is a ubiquitous problem, owing to the inability of human earning capacity to be collateralised. Second, poor families in particular face enormous barriers to the acquisition of debt, including uncertain future health and employment status and the large burden that servicing such debts would place on limited incomes. In any event, as a matter of social equity, we would prefer to see reductions in child labour and investments in human capital as social objectives, not tied to the degree of impoverishment to which large portions of the world's people are currently subjected. Instead, as we shall discuss shortly, our approach is to propose income transfer programmes that would address financial constraints at the household level without the accumulation of debt.

Before proceeding to a detailed description of the methodology, it is important to stress the limited objectives of the study. It is not a cost-benefit analysis (CBA) in the conventional sense. In principle, a CBA encompasses all factors that bear upon policy judgments; an excess of costs over benefits means "stop" and the reverse means "go". This requires the CBA analyst to convert all the consequences of a proposed course of action to

---

[1] See Basu and Van (1998), for instance, for a model in which multiple child labour equilibria coexist in an economy, and in which there is a case for collective action to move the society from a less- to more-desirable path.

[2] See Ranjan (2001), Dehejia and Gatti (2002) and Beegle et al. (2003).

monetary equivalents. In the current study, we are not doing this. As we shall see, only a subset of the consequences of eliminating child labour is modelled, and we make no effort to be fully inclusive. We would describe this exercise as an estimation of the economic *aspects* of eliminating child labour up to the extent permitted by the available data. We intend it to be one among many inputs into decision-making. In particular, in accordance with the approach embodied in Conventions No. 138 and No. 182, we view the economic benefits of eliminating child labour as one component of the larger social benefits. We would support this elimination even if the results of the study show that there are net economic costs, just as many other choices in life are justified even if they do not pay for themselves in solely economic terms. Of course, if it appears that permitting child labour to continue is economically costly, this will suggest that more aggressive elimination programmes are feasible, and that social objectives, in this case, do not need to be traded off against economic ones.

SUMMARY OF THE METHODOLOGY

Our study attempts to calculate the economic costs and benefits of the elimination of child labour, with specific results for the various forms of child labour, different sectors of society and different national and regional entities. In a general sense, the project considers the elimination of child labour as an investment and calculates its economic return. In doing so, it suggests the commitment of resources necessary to achieve this elimination, and it indicates how the costs and benefits accrue to different stakeholders.

Because the full complement of data required for such an analysis is not available at the global level, we opted for a two-stage process. In the first stage, eight countries were selected for their representativeness of different regions and levels of development, and for the availability of data on child labour: Nepal, Philippines, Pakistan, Kenya, Tanzania, Senegal, Brazil and Ukraine. Teams in each country tried to fill in the data gaps through uncovering sources of information not known or utilized internationally, as well as through surveys of knowledgeable informants and direct estimation. Based on this, they implemented country-level studies of costs and benefits. A second set of countries, while not intensively studied, offered more detailed information as a result of hosting household surveys. Many of these surveys were assisted by IPEC in conjunction with its SIMPOC programme or the World Bank as part of its LSMS (Living Standards Measurement Survey) programme; others were developed by national statistical offices. Thus, between these two types of data sources, we had between 8 and 28 observations on all variables measurable by survey methods. (Details for each variable can be found in Annex 2.) For the remainder of the countries we relied on publicly available data, most commonly from the World Bank's

World Development Indicators (WDI) data set. As described more fully in Annex 2, the largely complete WDI and related data were used to extrapolate from the first two sets of countries (those studied in conjunction with this project and those with household surveys) to the third.

While the project was ambitious, the time frame was condensed, so the methodological framework seeks a middle ground between completeness and simplicity. It focuses on three sources of cost – the cost of providing a quality education to all children in lieu of work, the cost of programme interventions to alter attitudes and practices, and the opportunity cost of eliminating this work, i.e. the value of children's labour. A central feature of this study is the hypothetical implementation of an income transfer programme in every country. The purpose of such a programme would be to indemnify poor families for a portion of the value of child labour foregone as a result of its elimination. As we will discuss in Chapter 5, only the administrative portion of this programme is a true economic cost, although the much larger transfer amounts have important effects on the distribution of costs and benefits to households and the public sector. On the benefit side, we calculate economic gains from a more educated and healthier population, with the latter resulting from the elimination of the worst forms of child labour. Calculations were based, whenever possible, on direct measurements from sources such as IPEC's Statistical Information and Monitoring Programme on Child Labour (SIMPOC), the World Bank's Living Standards Measurement Survey (LSMS), and national or local surveys and censuses. Where numbers had to be constructed or imputed, simpler methods were generally preferred to more complex ones.

The study models a process taking place over 20 years beginning in 2001 and calculates the present value in 2000 of the costs and benefits associated with this time period. Specifically, the model proposes to achieve full enrolment and attendance of all children in primary school by the end of 2015 and in lower secondary school by 2020. It would eliminate the worst forms on a more accelerated schedule, to be completed in 2010. Expenditures to achieve these goals are tracked on a year-by-year basis and summed and discounted to arrive at a present value. Similarly, the opportunity cost of foregone child labour is calculated for each year during this 20-year period and reported as a present value. The health benefits are calculated on the basis of impairments that would be prevented during these 20 years as the worst forms are eliminated, bearing in mind that long-lived impairments (including premature death) entail costs that extend beyond 2020. Similarly, the education benefits encompass the gains anticipated over the entire future work life of child beneficiaries. Hence, both benefits apply to the years of child labour eliminated or education expanded during the period 2001-2020, but incorporate effects based on years well beyond this cut-off point.

While each year is calculated individually, for reporting purposes the study was structured as a series of "waves". A wave is assumed to take place over a five-year period, and each wave begins as the preceding one ends.

So, wave 1 begins in 2001 during which one-third of the children ages 6 to 11 initially out of school will be enrolled in school, one-fourth of the poor children will be part of an income transfer programme, and 50% of the worst form of child labour will be prevented. In 2006, wave 2 closes an additional third of 6 to 11-year-old children's attendance gap and an initial third of the 12 to 14-year-old children's attendance gap. In addition, the income transfer programme will now reach half of the poor children, and all the worst forms of child labour will be eliminated. Wave 3 starts in 2011, completing the process of closing the attendance gap of 6 to 11-year-old children and closing the gap by another third for the 12 to 14 year-olds, while providing transfer funds to tree-fourths of poor children. Finally, in wave 4, which starts in 2016, the model envisions all children in school and all poor children subsidized by transfers. Essentially, then, each wave consolidates the annual changes taking place according to the projections established in the model.

Because this process takes place over a 20-year period, discounting is required to convert future values to their present equivalents. To this end, a real discount rate (r) of 5% was employed together with a set of growth rates (g) based on demographic projections. There are complications involving discounting, however, that we will address later in this chapter.

Based on the assumption that children are engaged in full-time work either because there are no schools at all within a convenient distance, or the schools are of such low quality that parents cannot see the advantage of enrolling their children, the costs of the supply side of education were computed, involving school quality as well as quantity. To obtain the costs of achieving universal primary and lower secondary education, the number of children out of school was multiplied by the expenditure per pupil. The costs required for lowering the student-to-teacher ratio to an average of 40:1 and purchases of material sufficient to reach the objective of 15% of overall recurrent education expenditures were used to obtain an estimate of the expenditures that would improve school quality. Moreover, capital expenditures necessary to have enough school establishments for achieving the goal of universal coverage were calculated.

Besides having enough school establishments and education of sufficient quality, parents must be able to overcome the purely economic barriers to having their children engaged in study. This includes the direct cost of schooling, such as books and uniforms, but also, and especially, the opportunity cost, or the value of the work children might have to give up if they increase their school participation. Based on this, in addition to the opportunity costs of the children's work, the cost of the demand side of education was calculated. These costs involve income transfer programme tied to school attendance when households' income is below poverty line. All school age children coming from poor families would receive a percentage of their opportunity cost of work. Finally, we envisaged the need for an array of interventions targeting children who might not be reached through either education expansion or income transfers. These include in the first instance all children engaged in the worst forms of child labour, since this work must be eliminated as a matter of priority and cannot wait for other processes to run their course. Specifically, we propose an intervention programme designed to remove children from all such situations within the first ten years. Second, we expect that children subject to social exclusion may require extra attention, and this will provide an additional purpose for targeted interventions. Finally, some children may be steered toward unsuitable work or away from education due to cultural factors that need to be addressed through such interventions as awareness-raising. This category would include programmes that target gender-specific factors, which are otherwise not formally incorporated in the model. In the study methodology, we do not distinguish between these different motives or gender of the targeted children and simply multiply the number of all children identified as falling into one of these three categories by the yearly expenditure per child based on the experience of existing child labour programmes.

To obtain the benefits of education, the present value of increased lifetime income attributable to greater educational attainment was measured. To this end, the total number of children out of school was multiplied by the Mincerian coefficient (marginal effect of an extra year of education on wage), and by unskilled adults' wages.

The results encompassed 152 countries divided into 5 regions, based on the groupings developed by the ILO's Key Indicators of the Labour Market (KILM), and as adjusted for consistency with the World Bank: Transitional countries (26 countries), Asia (32 countries), Latin America (29 countries), Sub-Saharan Africa (43 countries), North Africa & Middle East (22 countries). High-income countries were not considered due to a lack of access to data, especially considering that their patterns of child labour may differ from those found elsewhere (Dorman, 2001). Turkey, included among the developed countries in the KILM schema, was retained due to its value as the host of a SIMPOC survey; for accounting purposes it was transferred to the North Africa & Middle East region. Slovenia was dropped from the list of transitional countries, because we considered it a fully developed economy.

Data at the national level, except for a few of the study countries mentioned above, are incomplete. Nevertheless, the study methodology requires calculation at the national level. Typically, various national-level variables, such as population, income and wages, and educational or health conditions, are combined in the formulas for economic costs and benefits. This precludes working with regional averages. To overcome this problem, we used the observations derived from country studies, household surveys and other credible sources, along with economic and demographic variables for which complete (or nearly complete) series were available, to impute the missing observations required. The principal method was regression analysis, supplemented by the trimming of outliers and the estimation of residual cases by neighbourhood approximation. (As a last resort, we duplicated the relevant value from a nearby country with similar socio-economic conditions.) Annex 2 provides detailed description and analysis of every imputation employed in the study.

Individual country totals derived from imputation are less reliable, however, than their regional aggregates, since errors are largely asystematic. (Some country estimates will be too large, others too small, but the sum will be closer to hypothetical "true" values.) Consequently, we report only the regional and global totals. Of these, it should be noted that the results for the transitional countries and North Africa and the Middle East are somewhat less reliable, in the first case because this region encompasses a wide range of levels of development, and in the second because of the lack of an intensive country-level study. Concise summaries of three country studies developed during the first phase of this project, each representing one of the remaining regions, are included as annexes.

KEY RESULTS

Table 2.1 reports our baseline results, against which potential changes in the methodology and assumptions of our model will be compared. Figure 2.1 displays the net economic benefits as a percentage of regional and global aggregate national income. Table 2.2 provides more detail on the row headings employed.

Table 2.1. Total economic costs and benefits of eliminating child labour over the entire period (2000 to 2020), in $billion, PPP (Percentage of aggregate annual gross national income in parentheses)

Region	Transitional countries	Asia	Latin America	Sub-Saharan Africa	North Africa and Middle East	Global
Total costs	25.6	458.8	76.6	139.5	59.7	760.3
Education supply	8.5	299.1	38.7	107.4	39.6	493.4
Transfer implementation	0.7	6.3	1.2	1.5	1.1	10.7
Interventions	0.4	2.4	5.8	0.6	0.2	9.4
Opportunity cost	16.0	151.0	30.9	30.1	18.8	246.8
Total benefits	149.8	3 321.3	407.2	723.9	504.1	5 106.3
Education	145.8	3 307.2	403.4	721.8	500.2	5 078.4
Health	4.0	14.0	3.8	2.1	3.9	28.0
Net economic benefits	**124.2** **(5.1 %)**	**2 862.4** **(27.0%)**	**330.6** **(9.3%)**	**584.4** **(54.0%)**	**444.4** **(23.2%)**	**4 346.1** **(22.2%)**
Transfer payments	13.1	125.8	23.5	29.1	22.1	213.6
Net financial benefits	**111.1** **(4.6%)**	**2 736.6** **(25.9%)**	**307.1** **(8.7%)**	**555.4** **(51.3%)**	**422.3** **(22.0%)**	**4 132.5** **(21.1%)**

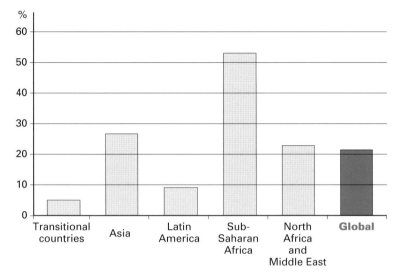

Figure 2.1. Net economic benefits as a percentage of annual Gross National Income

Table 2.2. Economic categories

Opportunity cost	Opportunity cost of child labour, the value of child labour foregone due to its elimination
Transfer programme	The administrative cost of the income transfer programme to promote the demand for education
Interventions	The cost of programme interventions targeting children in the worst forms of child labour or who experience social exclusion
Education supply	The cost of expanding the quantity and quality of education
Education benefits	The economic benefits anticipated from children receiving additional years of schooling at upgraded levels of quality
Health benefits	The economic benefits of improved health outcomes due to the elimination of the worst forms of child labour
Net economic benefits	The net economic benefits of eliminating child labour; total benefits minus total costs
Transfer payments	The income to be transferred to poor households with school-age children to promote the demand for education
Net financial benefits	Net economic benefits minus transfer payments, a measure of the financial reward (burden) of eliminating child labour

As can be seen, the global benefits of the elimination of child labour and the redirection of these children to education greatly exceed the costs. This result is so strong that it is unlikely that any plausible adjustment to the methodology would reverse it. As reported above, the study shows the present value of benefits in excess of costs approaches $4.5 trillion, and this pattern is replicated in each of the five regions. The principal benefit is, not surprisingly, the economic boost that most countries would experience if all children were educated through lower secondary school. The health benefit is far smaller, although, as we shall demonstrate in Chapter 8, this amount is almost certainly underestimated.

Unfortunately, achieving these large economic gains is not painless. Countries face two main difficulties. First, the expenses they must bear are up front, whereas the benefits accrue over several decades. Specifically, the education benefits first appear in 2006 and accumulate over the following 61 years. (We will investigate this problem in detail in Chapter 9.) Second, the income transfer programme at the heart of this study's model shifts over $200 billion to low-income families over the period 2000-2020 (on a present value basis). While this is not a resource cost in the economic sense, it is a financial burden on governments, and one many would be unable to bear without external assistance.

In subsequent chapters we will subject these results to sensitivity analysis, considering the effect of alternative assumptions on the individual cost and benefit components. Here we consider just one overall alternative, namely revisions to the discount rate r. There are two important issues associated with the determination of r. First, there is disagreement over the criteria for establishing discount rates in studies such as this, with the common sense position being that no single rate can adequately represent all the effects associated with the passage of time. We choose 5% because it is conventional in a wide range of studies. The second problem is more difficult to resolve. Most of the projections in this study are expressed as percentages of some economic variable, such average wages or unit costs of supplying education. If these grow over time, so do the values tied to them, such as the costs and benefits of expanded education. Technically, such growth would be expressed as a deduction from r. For example, suppose that r is set at 5%, and that we are measuring the cost of education. If this cost rises by 2% in real (inflation-adjusted) terms, and if the cost in the current period is $100, the present value of next year's cost is $97.14, rather than $95.24, which would be the amount if costs were constant. Specifically, for a discount rate of r and a growth rate of the underlying variable g, the adjusted discount rate is $(r-g)/(1+g)$. In our example this comes to 2.94%.

To see the role that this adjustment of effective r would play in this study, let us recalculate the costs and benefits of eliminating child labour when r is set at 2.94%. That is, let us assume that all relevant underlying economic magnitudes – per capita income, wages, personnel and materials costs, the value of child labour, the poverty line – increase in every country at the uniform real rate of 2% per year for the entire duration of the study period. Our new results matrix would appear as in Table 2-3.

All magnitudes increase, of course, but those that depend most on events well in the future increase the most. The cost of supplying education,

Table 2.3. Costs and benefits of eliminating child labour with r = 2.94%, in $billion PPP (Percentage of aggregate gross national income in parentheses)

Region	Transitional countries	Asia	Latin America	Sub-Saharan Africa	North Africa and Middle East	Global
Total costs	32.5	584.8	97.3	179.4	76.5	970.4
Education supply	10.7	378.9	49.6	137.6	50.4	627.3
Transfer implementation	0.9	8.5	1.6	2.0	1.5	14.4
Interventions	0.4	2.6	6.1	0.6	0.2	10.0
Opportunity cost	20.5	194.8	39.9	39.2	24.3	318.7
Total benefits	253.9	5 627.0	659.3	1 247.9	854.3	8 642.4
Education	248.9	5 609.3	654.5	1 245.2	849.4	8 607.2
Health	5.0	17.6	4.8	2.7	5.0	35.1
Net economic benefits	**221.4** **(9.1%)**	**5 042.2** **(47.7%)**	**562.0** **(15.9%)**	**1 068.5** **(98.7%)**	**777.8** **(40.6%)**	**7 671.9** **(39.3%)**
Transfer payments	17.7	169.6	31.7	39.2	29.8	288.0
Net financial benefits	**203.7** **(8.4%)**	**4 872.6** **(46.1%)**	**530.3** **(15.0%)**	**1 029.3** **(95.1%)**	**748.0** **(39.0%)**	**7 384.0** **(37.8%)**

the largest debit item, increases by just over 27%, while the education benefits increase by nearly 70%. Since the 5% discount rate used in the baseline results is predicated on no change in real economic variables, it is apparent that net benefits are depressed by this highly conservative assumption.

While the sensitivity of the model to other changes in assumptions remains to be explored (this will be undertaken in the following chapters), it is evident that the primary result – that the elimination of child labour is advantageous in solely economic terms – is not likely to be overturned. This demonstrates that doing the right thing for children, an imperative derived from humanitarian values, is also consistent with economic criteria. It shows that the world cannot only afford to do this; it can hardly afford not to. But it also shows that it will take global cooperation and forward-looking leadership to overcome the economic obstacles in the way of this goal.

In the following chapters, we will examine the various components of the results, looking in more detail at the different methodological tools applied in each case and discussing the sensitivity of the results.

WHO ARE THE CHILD WORKERS?

3

CHILD LABOUR TARGETED FOR ELIMINATION

The ILO's Minimum Age Convention, 1973 (No. 138), states that the minimum age for entry into employment should not be less than the age of completion of compulsory schooling, and not less than 15 years, or 14 in the case of countries "whose economy and educational facilities are insufficiently developed" (Article 2, paragraphs 3 and 4.) Accordingly, work that interferes with this education, either through direct substitution or through excessive hours, is prohibited. Hence, for this report, we counted all economically active children aged 5 to 11, considering their work as child labour that ought to be eliminated.

The situation is not so clear-cut for children aged 12 to 14, because Convention No. 138, Article 7, paragraph 1, permits light work for 13 to 14 year-olds (or 12 to 13 year-olds in developing countries).[1] Such light work should (a) not be harmful to a child's health and development and (b) not prejudice attendance at school and participation in vocational training nor "the capacity to benefit from the instruction received". What does this mean in statistical terms? Keeping close to recent ILO child labour estimates (ILO 2002) we considered as light work by children aged 12 to 14 that which is not hazardous in nature and which does not exceed 14 hours per week.[2] Consequently, the country-specific number of children in light work had to be subtracted from the national total of economically active 12 to 14 year-olds, and then added to the remaining number of 5 to 11 year-olds.

---

[1] In our model, we opt for 15 as a minimum age of work, anticipating the development of the latter group of countries, and 12 as the minimum age for light work.

[2] This threshold is one of several cut-off points available from SIMPOC national household surveys and was used in ILO (2002), in line with ILO Convention No. 33. Ongoing research is expected to generate a larger pool of information on which to base assessments of the impact of different levels of hours of work per week in various occupations on children's educational participation and performance.

In addition to the children whose labour should be eliminated because of their age, millions of children worldwide are entrapped in the worst forms of child labour, which should be eliminated "as a matter of urgency", as the ILO's Worst Forms of Child Labour Convention, 1999 (No.182) stipulates. Thus, the worst forms concern all children below the age of 18, including those above the minimum age of work.

COLLECTING CHILD LABOUR DATA

Data about children and their lives are still inadequate. Children are often effectively excluded from official statistics, which tend to focus on adults or formal institutions rather than on children. For example, children may be merely counted as members of households or as students in schools. Even where data on children are available, they may not be disaggregated by sex, age or other groupings, which would allow an understanding of the differences in situations and needs between these groups. Different government agencies often collect information for distinct purposes, using various age groupings, methods and time periods, so that the data sometimes cannot be centrally managed, shared or compared. National-level statistics are frequently not disaggregated to the levels at which programme interventions are planned and implemented (e.g. districts, sectors or villages) and this makes it difficult to undertake proper needs assessment, to target interventions and to evaluate their impact.

The ILO has made considerable strides over the years in assisting member States and other partners to collect and disseminate information about child labour, using innovative research methods. Since 1979, when a large number of country studies were commissioned for the International Year of the Child, there has been an ongoing programme of child labour research providing new insights through counting, describing and analysing the work of children in a variety of economic settings. This work was given a boost in 1998 with the launch of the Statistical Information and Monitoring Programme on Child Labour (SIMPOC) within IPEC. SIMPOC assists ILO member States in collecting information on children's work through national household surveys and a variety of other data collection efforts.

WORKING CHILDREN AGED 5 TO 14: RESULTS

For this report, data from 28 national household surveys were available and used for extrapolations, constituting the same data sets employed in *Every Child Counts* (ILO, 2002). We adopted the same adjustments to these data: for age rebracketing, standardization on year 2000, and discrepancies between SIMPOC and non-SIMPOC surveys.[3] Our extrapolation procedure was similar but not identical. Due to apparent differences in survey methodology, the observations did not prove amenable to extrapolation via regression, so we applied the unweighted regional average of the ratio of working to all children aged 5 to 14 to countries without surveys. The results are as follows:

Table 3.1. Working children aged 5 to 14 in thousands, using unweighted regional averages

Region	Total	Percent of Cohort
Transition countries	8 310	14.6
Asia	110 390	18.7
Latin America	16 466	17.0
Sub-Saharan Africa	37 902	25.3
North Africa and Middle East	9 027	10.2
Total	**182 096**	**18.5**

The third column reports working 5 to 14 year-olds as a percentage of the entire age group. According to the data available to us, the incidence of child labour varies greatly across regions, with the greatest concentration in sub-Saharan Africa. Indeed, this regional average might be regarded as an outlier, except that it is drawn from the largest number of household surveys.

It may be observed that our estimates of the incidence of child labour closely approximate those reported in *Every Child Counts*. Thus, the global total of child labourers in that document is 186.3 million, only slightly higher than ours. The discrepancy is attributable primarily to differences in the country composition; the current study excludes the developed countries and a few others for which economic and demographic data were not available.

In addition to comparing the global totals, it is useful to compare the regional composition. Here a direct comparison is not possible, because the current study excludes children ages 12 to 14 in light work (less than 14 hours per week), while *Every Child Counts* provides regional aggregates only for the more expansive category of economically active children, which

---

[3] For details, consult the first two appendices to ILO (2002).

Table 3.2. Percentage distribution of child labour and child economic activity, ages 5 to 14, across regions

Region	Child labour	Child economic activity
Transition countries	4.6	1.2
Asia	60.6	61.1
Latin America	9.0	8.3
Sub-Saharan Africa	20.8	23.0
North Africa and Middle East	5.0	6.4
Total[a]	**100.0**	**100.0**

[a] Total child economic activity excludes the developed countries.

Sources: Current study (child labour), Every Child Counts (child economic activity)

includes light work. Nevertheless, the distribution is broadly similar, as Table 3.2 demonstrates.

Differences can once again be explained by somewhat different country compositions of regions, as well as by differences in the extent of light work across regions. In either formulation, however, well more than half of all child labour or economic activity is accounted for by Asia and the Pacific, and more than half the remainder by Sub-Saharan Africa.

Behind these regional averages lie substantial differences at the country level. One of the countries providing input into this study was Nepal. According to its National Child Labour Survey (assisted by SIMPOC), of the 6.2 million children ages 5 to 14, nearly 2.6 million, or 41.6%, were engaged in some form of work. Of these, 1.7 million were working for remuneration. Clearly, child labour in Nepal is far more common that the 18.7% regional average for Asia would suggest. Thus, care should be taken in drawing inferences from average regional incidence rates; variation within regions is as substantial as variation across them.

THE WORST FORMS OF CHILD LABOUR

These extremely exploitative activities can be classified into (a) hazardous work and (b) the unconditional worst forms of child labour.

Hazardous work by children is any activity or occupation which, by its nature or type, has, or leads to, adverse effects on the child's safety, health (physical or mental), and moral development. Hazards could also derive from excessive workload, physical conditions of work, and/or work intensity in terms of the duration or hours of work even where the activity or occupation is known to be non-hazardous or safe. In principle, the number of children ages 15 to 17 engaged in hazardous work should be added to the child labour population ages 5 to 14 to arrive at a complete estimate of the extent of child labour. We do not do that in this study because the main role of our child labour total is to serve as an input into the calculation of opportunity costs. Hazardous work performed by older children presents a different problem, however, because its eradication would not typically entail an opportunity cost: children would be transferred from hazardous to non-hazardous activities, with no necessary loss in production or pay. Hence, for purposes of calculating opportunity costs, our measure of child labour does not include the 15 to 17 age group. On the other hand, we have, as Chapter 8 explains, incorporated a measure of the older age group in our calculation of the health benefits of eliminating child labour.

Hazardous work for all children's age groups also figures into our calculation of programme intervention costs. As we discuss more fully in Chapter 6, it is assumed that particular programmes will be required to remove child from such work, alter the work so as to make it no longer hazardous, or rehabilitate children who have experienced harm as a result of their hazard exposures. For purposes of consistency, in this context we do not extrapolate to create regional or global totals for hazardous work; we simply add up the existing observations, as is the case for other worst forms as well. The data were taken from the country tabulations used to construct *Every Child Counts,* which in turn were based on the numbers of children in mining, construction and a list of detailed occupations, as well as those working excessive hours. These were supplemented by the number of children working in mining and construction in countries for which more detailed information was unavailable (and which were therefore not used in *Every Child Counts*). Table 3.3 reports our data for hazardous work by region.

No particular significance should be attached to these numbers. They largely reflect the extent to which surveys in the various regions incorporated questions on the detailed industry and occupation of child workers.

For the purpose of this exercise, we considered children in forced and bonded labour, armed conflict, prostitution and pornography, and illicit

Table 3.3. Number of children in hazardous work by region, ages 5 to 14 (in thousands), underlying this study

Region	Hazardous work
Transitional countries	–
Asia and Pacific	5 078
Latin America	4 587
Sub-Saharan Africa	751
North Africa and Middle East	420
Global	**10 836**

activities[4] as **unconditional worst forms of child labour**. Trafficked children were excluded from the calculations in order to avoid double-counting. The figures for the unconditional worst forms of child labour are based on a comprehensive secondary data review, involving data collection, data validation, data selection and calculation of the global estimates.[5] When no reliable figure was found for a country, it does not appear in our calculations; unlike the other variables used in our calculations, no extrapolation from one country to another was made. This is because the observations, where they exist, are based on identified populations and are themselves not generally representative of the complete counts that would be obtained through comprehensive surveys. Therefore, the results in Table 3.4, based on available data from 56 countries, should be considered as conservative minimum estimates. Columns 2 through 4 provide low, medium and high estimates, based on uncertainties regarding the totals in specific countries.

Table 3.4. Children in the unconditional worst forms of child labour, ages 5 to 17 (in thousands)

Region	Low	Medium	High
Transitional countries	9	9	9
Asia and Pacific	6581	12691	18450
Latin America	887	952	1018
Sub-Saharan Africa	689	770	851
North Africa and Middle East	71	71	71
Total	**8236**	**14492**	**20398**

It has to be noted that national micro data sets on unconditional worst forms on child labour are almost non-existent. This is an area where there is an urgent need for the development of appropriate survey instruments. Given the limited evidence at present, the above figures are likely to underestimate the true extent of the unconditional worst forms of child labour in the 56 countries where data were available. Moreover, children in these countries account for only 56% of the total child population in developing and transitional countries. In other words, no data at all exist on countries that harbour 44% of the children that should in principle be surveyed for this study. While in the case of some worst forms of child labour, such as

---

[4] For a definition of these terms, see ILO (2002).
[5] For an in-depth description of these steps, see ILO (2002).

child soldiers or bonded labourers, it is fairly easy to exclude several countries from the list, there is every reason to believe that the number of children involved in the other unconditional worst forms (e.g. sexual exploitation or illicit activities) is not zero in the remaining countries. Nevertheless, we did not have a basis for extrapolation, because our country totals do not represent reliable estimates of the true number of children engaged in these forms of exploitation but rather confirmed populations, and the discrepancy between these two varies unsystematically across countries.

From a programme point of view, addressing these unconditional worst forms presents a particular challenge, as they are often hidden and/or related to some form of social exclusion or stigma. Hence, the children involved in these activities will not be easily integrated into the formal school system. It is clear that a sustainable withdrawal from their exploitative work situations will require specific, targeted interventions to overcome social and cultural obstacles to school attendance (see Chapter 6).

Since ILO Convention No. 182 calls for the *urgent* elimination of the worst forms of child labour, our model envisages their effective elimination over a ten-year period, that is, during the first two waves.

THE COST OF INCREASING THE QUANTITY AND QUALITY OF EDUCATION

4

EDUCATION AS AN ALTERNATIVE TO CHILD LABOUR

ILO Convention No. 138 links the minimum age for work to the age of completion of compulsory schooling. By establishing such a link, the aim is to ensure that children's human capital is developed to its fullest potential, benefiting children themselves, their families and communities and society as a whole by the increased contribution they can, when grown, make to economic growth and social development.

Education is indeed the most compelling potential alternative to full-time work for children. Millions of children are engaged in full-time work because a satisfactory alternative is not available to them: either there are no schools at all within a convenient distance, or the schools are of such low quality that parents cannot see the advantage of enrolling their children. Even if children do attend such sub-standard schools, they may not receive the benefits that ought to be available to them as a result of foregoing child labour. 12 to 14-year-old students of such schools, who are permitted to combine schooling and light work, might regard their out-of-school time better spent working excessive hours than preparing their homework. For these reasons, quality as well as quantity (and location) are central to education supply. Finally, formal enrolment alone is not sufficient for realizing the benefits of education; actual attendance is required as well.

METHODOLOGY

Research teams in the eight study countries applied the following methodology.

The first step was to ascertain the physical accessibility of primary and lower secondary education. Accessibility is a function of mobility, of course. In an area in which people travel mostly on foot the accessibility radius of a school is smaller than in one in which people can travel by other forms of transport. In addition, a degree of capacity sufficient to serve a portion of the relevant age cohort is not the same as that needed to serve all such children, including those not currently attending.

Second, the country teams determined how many children have access to some form of age-appropriate school, but lack access to *quality* education. This is a difficult and controversial question to answer (Matz, 2003). There is no universally agreed-upon set of criteria for quality; different analysts have different approaches. Quality may not mean the same thing in one country as another, since the challenges set before the school system may differ. Moreover, any dividing line between "adequate" and "inadequate" quality is necessarily arbitrary, and observers may disagree about where it should be drawn. Despite these qualifications, the following criteria were applied:

o   Pupil-to-teacher ratio: this should not exceed 40 for any school. This seems to be a necessary, albeit not sufficient condition for the provision of quality education (Mehrotra/Vandemoortele, 1997). Prescribing such a ratio on a national basis is a conservative minimum requirement, as a national average of 40 would presumably include many schools that fail to meet this standard.

o   Books and other teaching materials: non-salary recurrent costs must not be less than 15% of overall recurrent expenditure. At least until minimum thresholds have been exceeded, additional learning materials have been found to be priority to improving school quality in developing countries (Colclough/Lewin, 1993; Wolff et al., 1994). Allocating 15% of total recurrent expenditure is a benchmark derived from developed countries' education budgets (Delamonica et al., 2001).

Even though they are to some extent arbitrary, these measures have the advantage of not only identifying such quality gaps as may exist, but also providing a method for calculating the cost of closing them. Thus the formula used to determine quality upgrade was:

$$\text{Quality upgrade cost} = \text{additional salary cost to achieve}$$
$$\text{minimum pupil-to-teacher ratio} + \text{additional non-salary costs}$$

An example of quality upgrade costs in the context of one of our study countries is provided by Kenya. In 2000 teachers' salaries comprised 97.2% of all recurrent costs in primary education, well above the quality guideline given above. In order for non-salary costs to account for 15% of the total, the 2000 expenditure must be increased more than fivefold. This was incorporated into our estimate for Kenya's future recurrent costs. Similarly, teacher salaries comprised 94.5% of secondary recurrent costs, requiring a corresponding quality adjustment.

Quality upgrade costs were expressed on a unit basis, that is, per student in the relevant target population. It was not always possible to differentiate between unit costs for primary and lower secondary schools, as teacher salaries, the most important determinant of unit costs, vary greatly according to age, qualification and location and were not reported in detail in most of the study countries. Moreover, attendance data is reported on the basis of national school norms, and different school systems have different age break-ups, which means that the ratio of primary to lower secondary for students below the age of 15 varies greatly across countries. Thus, a single unit cost was usually prescribed for quality upgrades at both levels.[1]

Where no education existed before, the existing recurrent unit costs (cumulative) and capital unit costs (non-cumulative) of supplying education were applied, and the upgrade costs added. In addition, the country teams were asked whether a sufficient infrastructure (e.g. teacher training facilities) to support the provision of quality education were available. Where the answer was no, the cost results were multiplied times 1.25.

The country teams were alerted to the possibilities of economies or diseconomies of scale affecting the unit costs. However, no findings emerged that would have shed light on this question, so we assumed constant returns to scale.

In all calculations, the projected growth rate of the target population over time was taken into account.

DATA

The enrolment data reported by national Ministries of Education and by UNESCO have little relationship to actual attendance rates as measured by household surveys. Since, from both a child labour and an economic standpoint it is actual attendance that matters, we opted for the survey results. Specifically, we used the attendance series reported by UNICEF for 89 countries (*The State of the World's Children,* 2003) as a basis for extrapolation.

---

[1] Data collected by the UNESCO Institute for Statistics indicate that the expenditure per pupil in developing countries is only slightly higher in lower secondary school than in primary school (OECD/UNESCO, 2001). The reported ratio of lower secondary to primary expenditure per pupil corresponds roughly to the ratio of overall unit costs (recurrent *and* capital) between lower secondary and primary education in our calculations. Two caveats should be noted, however: the UNESCO sample was taken from middle-income countries whose teacher salary distributions may differ from that of lower-income countries, and within these sample averages are large variations in the second-to-primary ratios across countries.

These values were trimmed for the purpose of imputation, and the regional average was applied to the remaining countries, since there was relatively little variation within regions.

For lower secondary education, we used net attendance rates (denominated in the same fashion as net enrolment rates) collected in six of our country studies and added attendance rates from four SIMPOC national household surveys. The subsequent extrapolation was performed as a mix of neighbourhood imputations and assigning secondary-to-primary ratios from countries where data were available for both levels to countries where data were available only for the primary level. The resulting regional and global population-weighted averages are reported in Table 4.1.

The projection of education needs is complicated by expected changes in the population of the relevant age brackets over the duration of the model. In some countries, particularly in parts of Sub-Saharan Africa, North Africa and the Middle East, the number of children of primary or secondary school age is expected to increase significantly by 2020. This means that each year's expenditure must incorporate a growth factor, so that eliminating a constant fraction of the NAR gap translates into a rising cost over time. On the other hand, many countries anticipate population declines in this age group. This could be due either to reduced population overall or to a changing age profile. If the population of school-age children diminishes, this will be reflected initially in a declining expenditure in order to close a constant fraction of the NAR gap. In fact, it will probably be the case that capital expenditures will reach zero before the model's horizon has been reached. This is because spending on school increases the capacity of the education system to meet the needs of future students. At some point, this capacity can exceed the entire eligible population. (Box 4.1. illustrates this process using the example of Ukraine.) At the primary level, 68 countries in our sample reach this situation before the end of the 15 horizon, averaging 7.9 years of zero expenditure. For lower secondary the corresponding amounts are 60 countries and 6.6 years, reflecting lower initial attendance rates at this level.

Table 4.1. Net attendance rates by level and region

Region	Primary	Lower secondary
Transitional countries	89.5	84.7
Asia and Pacific	76.8	47.8
Latin America	91.4	49.4
Sub-Saharan Africa	56.4	27.8
North Africa and Middle East	82.3	62.7
Total	**76.2**	**48.9**

Box 4.1. Population decline and lower secondary education costs in Ukraine

The net attendance rate in Ukraine for children between the ages of 12 and 14 is .86. If we assume that the current ratio of schools to students must be maintained as attendance increases, this requires a spending programme on building new schools. The unit cost per student served by such schools is reported to be $4,475, and the population of children in this age bracket in 2005 is projected at just over 1.9 million. Thus, with one-fifteenth of the schooling gap to be made up in the first year of the second wave, the expenditure comes to approximately $80 million (undiscounted). But the population of 12 to 14 year-olds is expected to decline in Ukraine, arriving at only 1.1 million in 2020. This represents an annually compounded decrease of 3.7%.

The relevant information is summarized in the following table.

Table 4.2. Lower secondary school capacity
and student population in Ukraine

Year	Capacity	Population
Initial	1 659 737	1 940 131
1	1 677 742	1 868 677
2	1 696 435	1 799 854
3	1 713 776	1 733 567
4	1 730 479	1 669 721

The initial education capacity is assumed to be equal to the initial population times the attendance rate. The capacity rises in the first year of the second wave as a result of the spending on additional schools; meanwhile, the population being served falls. (Because of this decline, capital expenditures will be less in the second year of wave 2: $77.6 million.) With each subsequent year, money spent on building new schools leads to an increase in the capacity of the school system, while the decline in the number of students needing to be schooled reduces the gap. After three years, there is no need for further school-building, even if the population were fully enrolled. Hence, secondary education costs for Ukraine include 15 years of recurrent expenses but only three years of capital.

A rapidly diminishing population rate is characteristic of transitional countries: only one anticipates population growth, while three have rates of decline even greater than Ukraine's. By contrast, only two countries in Sub-Saharan Africa anticipate fewer 12-14 year-olds than at present.

The recurrent unit costs in the country studies consisted of current unit costs (as reported by the Ministries of Education), plus required quality improvement according to the criteria specified above, for which the underlying pupil-teacher ratios and non-salary expenditures were also gathered from the Ministries of Education. These were combined into an augmented unit recurrent cost total, which was then used as the basis for imputation to the rest of regions 2 to 6. The unit capital costs were calculated from the Ministries' of Education reported expenditure on buildings and equipment and the corresponding capacity to accommodate students. (We did not have sufficient data to distinguish between primary and secondary unit costs.)

Box 4.2. Direct costs of education

Three of our study countries reported significant education costs being borne by households. They are large enough to have a bearing on the prospective costs of achieving full attendance by 2020, and they constitute a potential disincentive on the demand side of education as well.

Pakistan

Public records do not distinguish between expenditures on primary and lower secondary schools, so the Pakistani researchers determined the recurrent cost at both levels by dividing the total amount spent on primary education by the number of students at the primary level. This amounted to $182 in PPP 2000. But households also pay directly for school, as revealed by a 1998 household survey. These direct costs averaged $68 for public primary school students and $150 for public secondary students in PPP 1998. Even considering that lower secondary students probably pay less in direct costs than those in higher grades, the importance of household contributions is striking.

Nepal

Government spending on public primary education averaged $170 per pupil in 2000. A 1996 survey, however, found that households paid the equivalent of $39 in direct costs (both in PPP 2000). Thus, the direct costs were 23% of the public expenditures.

Kenya

A 1994 survey found that public spending per pupil was $151 at the primary level and $507 at the secondary, but that the corresponding direct costs to the household were $56 and $620. Remarkably, the majority of expenses of secondary education were borne by students and their families. By the time a further survey was conducted in 1997, these costs had declined to $32 and $428 (in $PPP 1977), but they remained substantial.

Overall, it is clear that in many countries it is not enough to canvass government agencies to determine the amount spent on education. We include direct costs in our calculations of total expenditures for two reasons. First, it is an important component of the total resource cost envisioned for achieving full attendance. Second, we propose that, as part of the larger programme modelled in this study, the public sector should assume the full financial cost of education through the lower secondary level. Only in this way can the transfer programme considered in the following chapter be regarded as sufficient to achieve its demand-side objectives. Hence, we allocate direct costs to the public sector in our distributional analysis, even though they are currently paid by households.

Table 4.3. Average unit costs of education supply by type and region, in $PPP

Region	Recurrent	Capital		
		low	medium	high
Transitional countries	345	345	777	3 728
Asia and Pacific	295	295	663	3 183
Latin America	407	407	916	4 396
Sub-Saharan Africa	170	170	383	1 838
North Africa and Middle East	349	349	784	3 765
Total	**277**	**277**	**623**	**2 989**

In one instance, we adjusted recurrent costs to incorporate the project effects of HIV/AIDS. This disease strikes down adults, including teachers, during their prime productive years. Given the need for even more teachers to achieve full attendance and the cost of training them, it is likely that, among the other hardships resulting from this epidemic, there will be an increase in needed expenditures on education. Among our study countries, Kenya is seriously affected by the spread of HIV/AIDS, with a prevalence rate of 13.5% in 1999. We do not have a direct basis for inferring from this the likely burden on the country's educational system, but we do have this information for Mozambique, which can serve as a benchmark. Mozambique, with a 13.2% prevalence in 1999, has been estimated to face an increase of 6.79% in its cost of providing teachers for the public school system.[2] Extrapolating on the basis of relative prevalence rates, this translates to a 6.94% increase in Kenya. We did not perform this calculation for other African countries, but using Kenya as a partial basis for our global extrapolation embodied this effect indirectly. In the absence of other bases for projecting the future incidence of this disease, we made the conservative assumption that it would continue at its current level throughout the 20-year implementation period of our model. During the years of peak expenditure on the recurrent costs at the primary level in this model, 2015-2020, the results correspond roughly to the World Bank (2002) estimate that HIV/AIDS will add between $450 and $550 million per year to the cost of achieving universal education.[3]

An additional problem is raised by direct costs of education, defined as expenditures made by households directly to schools for the education of their children. These may include fees as well as purchases of books or other essential materials. The importance of these costs differs widely among the countries we studied, ranging from insignificant (Ukraine and Brazil) to substantial, as Box 4.2 demonstrates.

The extrapolation of these eight observations to the global level is described in Annex 2. A modest relationship between the ratio of unit recurrent costs to per capita income and per capita income itself was used to generate estimates on this variable to the remaining countries. There was no systemic relationship that could be used to a similar effect with unit capital costs, however. In lieu of this, we estimated low, medium and high capital costs based on the range of ratios of unit capital to recurrent costs in the eight study countries. The medium set of estimates is our baseline in this study, but Table 4.3 reports all three, along with unit recurrent costs. Regional averages are weighted by the number of children not attending school, as derived from age populations and estimated net attendance rates.

As can be seen, capital costs take the form of a multiple of recurrent costs. This multiple is 1, 2.25 and 4.8 respectively for low, medium and high estimates. (The regional averages in Table 4.3 do not reflect this precisely

---

[2] UNDP (2000).
[3] World Bank (2002).

because they include the eight countries that were recorded directly, rather than estimated.)

The most consequential estimates, from the standpoint of our education cost calculations, are the unit recurrent costs. There are two reasons for this. First, they are cumulative throughout the 20-year model period, whereas capital costs are one-time only. That is, a $1 increase in unit capital costs will be multiplied by the number of additional children for whom education is to be provided, whereas the same increase in unit recurrent costs will be multiplied by the number of children, and then multiplied again by the number of years this additional supply will be maintained. Second, we estimated unit capital costs as multiples of recurrent. How much room is there for underestimation of these recurrent costs? One way to cross-check our estimates is to compare them to teacher salaries. Drawing on the LABORSTA dataset (see Chapter 7 for details), we find 60 countries with observations on both average unskilled wages and average teacher salaries. (Two additional data points were deleted because they appeared implausible.) In Table 4.4 we report the average ratio of the teachers' to unskilled wages and the average annual teacher salary itself. Regional and global averages apply only to those countries for which we had data, and they were weighted by total population.

The World Bank's World Development Indicators, drawing on UN-ESCO's Institute for Statistics, provide data on average pupil teacher ratios in most countries. The population-weighted average for PTR in the countries in regions 2 to 6 is 27. Combining this information with the teacher salary data above, and bearing in mind that teacher salaries represent the largest portion of recurrent education costs, the estimates in Table 4.3 appear entirely plausible. At the global average, the teacher salary per student would come to $158, i.e. 57% of the corresponding unit recurrent cost. It is unlikely, then, that we are underestimating these costs to the degree that the overall conclusions of this study would be affected.

With this established, we will move to the total cost calculations themselves.

Table 4.4. Average teacher-to-unskilled wage ratio and average annual teacher salaries by region in $PPP

Region	Ratio of teacher to unskilled wages	Annual teacher salary
Transitional countries	0.93	4 598
Asia and Pacific	1.2	3 598
Latin America	2.31	7 967
Sub-Saharan Africa	3.51	6 273
North Africa and Middle East	2.40	7 305
Total	**1.45**	**4270**

Recurrent costs increase rapidly from wave to the next because they are cumulative, except for primary education in wave 4, since this last wave recapitulates the cost of the final year of wave 3, discounted at five additional years. The expansion of primary education entails greater costs, due to the larger number of grade levels and the extra wave of provision.

There are no capital costs in primary education in wave 4, since the model assumes that educational capacity will have expanded to include all children by that point. (We do not include an additional cost to accommodate possible school-age population increases during the final five years.) Note the substantial reduction in expenditures for both levels over time, due to the early attainment of full capacity in population-diminishing countries as well as the effect of discounting.

Comparing the four tables 4.5 through 4.8, several patterns emerge. Recurrent costs per wave are approximately the same for both levels, considering the role played by discounting. Capital costs are somewhat larger at the secondary level, even though they are discounted over an extra five years, due to differences in attendance rates. Also, the vast majority of all costs are accounted for by the educational needs of Asia and sub-Saharan Africa.

Table 4.5. Recurrent costs, primary education by region and wave, in $billion PPP (baseline calculation)

Region	Wave 1	Wave 2	Wave 3	Wave 4
Transitional countries	0.5	0.9	1.6	2.1
Asia and Pacific	11.9	23.1	45.8	61.0
Latin America	1.0	1.9	3.8	5.1
Sub-Saharan Africa	3.4	7.4	15.9	29.0
North Africa and Middle East	1.6	3.2	6.3	9.1
Total	**18.4**	**36.5**	**73.3**	**106.3**

Table 4.6. Recurrent costs, secondary education by region and wave, in $billion PPP (baseline calculation)

Region	Wave 2	Wave 3	Wave 4
Transitional countries	0.3	0.6	0.9
Asia and Pacific	10.4	20.2	39.0
Latin America	2.3	4.5	8.7
Sub-Saharan Africa	2.3	5.0	10.7
North Africa and Middle East	1.4	2.7	5.3
Total	**16.8**	**32.9**	**64.6**

Table 4.7. Capital costs, primary education by region and wave, in $billion PPP (baseline calculation)

Region	Wave 1	Wave 2	Wave 3
Transitional countries	0.8	0.1	0.0
Asia and Pacific	20.9	14.5	8.5
Latin America	1.5	1.1	0.7
Sub-Saharan Africa	6.0	5.2	4.5
North Africa and Middle East	2.4	1.9	1.1
Total	**31.6**	**22.8**	**14.8**

Table 4.8. Capital costs, secondary education by region and wave, in $billion PPP (baseline calculation)

Region	Wave 2	Wave 3	Wave 4
Transitional countries	0.6	0.1	0.0
Asia and Pacific	19.8	15.0	9.1
Latin America	3.5	2.7	1.9
Sub-Saharan Africa	6.9	6.0	5.1
North Africa and Middle East	2.1	1.7	1.0
Total	**32.8**	**25.4**	**17.1**

To sum up, we will consider the effects of substituting the low and high unit capital cost estimates for our baseline medium calculation. Table 4.9 compares the three possible costs of education by region based on these differing capital cost assumptions.

These costs increase at a increasing rate, since the recurrent component, which plays a more important role when capital costs are low, is fixed. It is pertinent to consider the effect of the highest assumptions about capital costs on our summary results. These are portrayed in Table 4.10.

Table 4.9. Education costs by region using low, medium and high unit capital cost assumptions, in $billion PPP

Region	Transitional countries	Asia	Latin America	Sub-Saharan Africa	North Africa and Middle East	Global
Low	8.0	266.0	34.2	95.9	34.0	438.0
Medium	8.6	299.1	38.7	107.4	39.6	493.4
High	9.8	366.8	47.8	131.0	51.1	606.3

The cost of increasing the quantity and quality of education

Table 4.10. Summary costs and benefits based on "high" estimates
of unit capital costs of education, in $billion PPP
(Percentage of aggregate national income in parentheses)

Region	Transitional countries	Asia	Latin America	Sub-Saharan Africa	North Africa and Middle East	Global
Total costs	26.9	526.5	85.7	162.9	71.2	873.2
Education supply	9.8	366.8	47.8	130.8	51.1	606.3
Transfer implementation	0.7	6.3	1.2	1.5	1.1	10.7
Intervention	0.4	2.4	5.8	0.6	0.2	9.4
Opportunity cost	16.0	151.0	30.9	30.1	18.8	246.8
Total benefits	149.8	3 321.3	407.2	723.9	504.1	5 106.3
Education	145.8	3 307.2	403.4	721.8	500.2	5 078.4
Health	4.0	14.0	3.8	2.2	3.9	28.0
Net economic benefits	**122.9** **(5.1%)**	**2 794.8** **(26.4%)**	**321.5** **(9.1%)**	**561.0** **(51.8%)**	**432.9** **(22.6%)**	**4 233.2** **(21.7%)**
Transfer payments	13.1	125.8	23.5	29.1	22.1	213.6
Net financial benefits	**109.8** **(4.5%)**	**2 669.0** **(25.2%)**	**298.0** **(8.4%)**	**532.0** **(49.2%)**	**410.8** **(21.4%)**	**4 019.6** **(20.6%)**

Net global benefits remain strongly positive, both globally and in every region. The difference between our baseline measures of the costs and benefits of expanding education is so large that plausible increases in these costs cannot alter the overall findings.

Returning to our baseline numbers, it may be observed that the unit costs estimated in this report are, on balance, substantially higher than those put forward by UNESCO. Table 4.11 provides the relevant comparisons:

This table reports the unit recurrent costs from this study and Scenario 2 of UNESCO, which incorporates adjustments for quality changes, along with average teacher salaries. (We converted the UNESCO estimates from 1995 to 2000 $PPP.) It is evident that, not only are our global estimates half

Table 4.11. Current average unit cost of education, $PPP (year 2000)

Region	Transitional countries	Asia	Latin America	Sub-Saharan Africa	North Africa and Middle East	Global
ILO-IPEC	345	295	407	170	349	277
UNESCO Scenario 2*	535	79	364	91	447	180
Teacher salaries	4 598	3 598	7 967	6 273	7 305	4 270

* Source: Brossard and Gacougnolle, forthcoming. Financing Primary Education for All: Yesterday, Today and Tomorrow, UNESCO.

45

again as large as UNESCO's, but there are even greater variations across regions. There are several differences in methodology that illuminate these comparisons:

1) Our study is based on the research performed in eight study countries, from which we extrapolated to the rest of the world. These were conducted by independent researchers familiar with local conditions. UNESCO obtained data from a larger number of countries, but these were survey responses by education ministries.

2) Our study separated out the capital costs, whereas UNESCO's did not. Thus the combined unit cost disparities would be greater than those reported in Table 4.11.

3) Our study included direct costs of education, which UNESCO's did not. As we have seen from Box 4.2, these are significant in many countries. Indeed, Sub-Saharan Africa and Asia are the two regions in which we found the greatest direct costs, and they are also the regions in which the ratio of our cost estimates to UNESCO's is the largest.

One way to evaluate these regional differences is to compare them to data on teacher salaries, row 4 in Table 4.11. These regional averages were computed from the LABORSTA data described above. We might suppose that education costs, particularly recurrent, will be roughly in proportion to these salaries. If so, we would be interested in the ratio of unit education costs to teacher salaries between regions. For instance, the average unit cost ratio for our study between the transitional countries and Asia is 345:295 or 1.17. The same ratio for UNESCO is 535:97 or 6.77. But the ratio of teacher salaries is 4598:3598 or 1.28. Assuming for the sake of analysis that the region-to-region teacher salary ratio is the correct benchmark, we can define either ILO's or UNESCO's error as the difference between its unit cost ratio for a given pair of regions and the corresponding ratio of teacher costs. To continue our example, the ILO error is –.11 and UNESCO's is 5.49. To put some perspective on these numbers, the absolute value of ILO's error is 8.5% of the potentially more reliable ratio of teacher salaries between these two regions, compared to 430% for UNESCO.

Over the five regions there are four fundamental ratios, in the sense that any other ratio can be expressed as a combination of these four. Here we will identify them as (region) 2:3, 3:4, 4:5 and 5:6. If we perform the above calculations for all four regional pairs, the ILO error is always less than UNESCO's; the average ILO error is 50% of the average teacher salary ratio, while the equivalent figure for UNESCO is 242%. Hence, to the extent that differences in teacher salaries are thought to correspond to differences in regional unit education costs, there is support for the estimates we use in this study.

A different way to compare our costs of education with other estimates is to look at the annual flows over the 20-year duration of the programme.

(For additional discussion of annual flow methodology, see Chapter 9 and Annex 3.) Table 4.12 tracks these undiscounted costs by region.

Recently, the World Bank published a detailed estimate of the cost of achieving universal primary school completion worldwide by 2015 (Bruns et al., 2003). The incremental cost, the difference between the expenditures required to achieve this goal and those currently financing primary education, amount to approximately $17.5 billion in the horizon year, just over a sixth of our corresponding amount. What explains such a large difference?

First, the two estimation exercises are not comparable. Our goal is to achieve universal *attendance* by this age group in 2015, whereas the Bank targets universal *completion*. Even more significant from a cost standpoint is the difference in methods for calculating the resources needed to expand education. The Bank advances a standard set of education supply criteria for implementation in all countries: universal pupil-to-teacher and to-classroom ratios of 40:1 (neither lower nor higher), best practice capital construction costs (which may differ from current costs), and a fixed range of teacher salaries (which entails raising them in some countries but lowering

Table 4.12. Annual undiscounted additional costs of education by region, in $billion PPP

Programme year	Region					Global
	Transitional countries	Asia	Latin America	Sub-Saharan Africa	North Africa and Middle East	
1	0.4	6.4	0.5	1.8	0.8	10.8
2	0.4	6.7	0.5	1.9	0.8	12.3
3	0.3	7.2	0.5	2.1	0.9	13.9
4	0.2	7.7	0.6	2.3	0.9	15.7
5	0.2	8.3	0.6	2.5	1.0	17.7
6	0.5	16.6	2.1	5.1	2.0	32.3
7	0.6	17.9	2.3	5.6	2.2	35.4
8	0.6	19.4	2.5	6.1	2.4	38.9
9	0.5	19.9	2.7	6.8	3.2	42.1
10	0.5	22.1	3.0	7.6	3.3	46.5
11	0.6	24.8	3.3	8.6	3.4	51.7
12	0.7	28.1	3.7	9.7	3.3	57.4
13	0.8	32.0	4.2	11.1	3.4	64.5
14	0.9	36.9	4.7	12.9	3.5	72.8
15	1.1	40.1	5.4	14.8	3.6	79.9
16	1.1	40.2	5.6	13.9	3.1	80.0
17	1.2	42.7	6.2	14.6	3.1	84.8
18	1.2	45.4	6.8	15.5	3.1	90.0
19	1.3	48.2	7.6	16.6	3.1	95.8
20	1.4	52.4	7.9	17.9	3.1	102.7

them in others). Our study, by contrast, extrapolates from existing unit capital and recurrent costs and assumes no change in PTR or the intensity of classroom use unless these figures are inordinately high.

Second, several of the Bank's methods have the effect of reducing their estimates relative to ours. The most important of these is their decision to use market exchange rates rather than purchasing power parity ratios to translate local currencies into US dollar equivalents.

Others include the option of designating five years as primary school duration in countries where this is the norm and incorporating the expectation that a portion of enrollment growth will be captured by the private sector, leaving it outside their cost model. Our study standardizes all countries on six years of primary school and assumes no expansion of private schooling.

Taken together, these differences in method roughly explain the differences in estimated costs.

THE DIRECT HOUSEHOLD COSTS OF ELIMINATING CHILD LABOUR

5

In the model employed by this study, households incur costs from the elimination of child labour, but also receive benefits. They forego the opportunity costs of withdrawing their children from work, namely the lost income or productivity in kind generated by them. In return, they receive income transfers according to the formula postulated by our model. Of course, these are not exactly the same households: non-poor households with child labourers incur only costs, while poor households whose children were not gainfully employed receive only benefits. We abstract from this issue, however, and treat the household sector as a single unit. We assume in doing so that non-poor families are generally able to bear the opportunity costs with their own resources, while transfers to poor families serve useful social purposes in addition to promoting the education and child labour goals of our model.

In this chapter, we will describe the methods used to estimate costs and benefits at the household level. Before doing this, however, we must first distinguish between economic costs and those which are financial but not economic. From the standpoint of economic theory, the only true costs of any course of action are opportunity costs (what could have been gained from using resources elsewhere rather than in a particular activity) and disutility (the direct unpleasantness of undertaking an activity). In conventional usage, however, costs refer to expenditures that need to be made in order to achieve some result. These are not the same, since some expenditures are not economic costs, and some economic costs are not expenditures. An example of the former would be an income transfer programme, such as we will describe, in which money is moved from one account (the government's) to another account (a poor family's), but there is no corresponding effect on real resources: no goods or services are directly foregone as a result of the transfer. (In principle, it is conceivable that the poor family could spend its new money on exactly the same items that the government would have chosen.) Of course, the *administrative* costs of the transfer programme are true economic costs, since the money paid for government employees compensates them for the disutility of their work as well as the loss of other possible uses of their time. Since income transfer programmes are expected to play an important role in the study, it is important to maintain this distinction. By measuring transfer and true economic (opportunity/disutility) costs separately, we can provide both an economic expression of these costs (what society gives up to pay them) and a fiscal expression (how great a burden these costs would place on private and public budgets).

An example of economic costs that are not expenditures would be the economic value of unpaid child labour. When a child takes care of a younger sibling or gathers firewood, for example, money is unlikely to change hands, but the activity has real economic consequences. Human needs – child-minding and fuel provision – that would otherwise go unmet are being serviced. It is essential to put an economic, which is to say a monetary, value on these activities. If children withdraw from some or all of these activities, either households will have to accept a lower level of self-provision or they will have to find some other people (other family members, other members of the community) to fill in. Of course, it is difficult to estimate the monetary equivalent for work that is neither paid nor leads to marketed output, but a tentative approach is made here.

Another point to be clarified is how the costs are distributed within the sectors. In this chapter we will discuss the costs and benefits to "households", but this is an incomplete account of how individuals within this sector will be affected. First, we include in this category only the household in which the child who is part of the target group now lives, and not the child's *future* household, particularly in the context of education benefits calculated over a 40 year time horizon. Second, we do not consider how costs and benefits will be apportioned among the individuals who make up these households. There is a substantial literature in the social sciences that considers the allocation of money and other goods within the household. This is far from a trivial issue, since in many countries unequal allocation at this level can have far-reaching consequences for health and human opportunities. Nevertheless, these refinements are beyond the scope of the present study, which must go to considerable lengths to estimate economic flows to and from households in the aggregate, much less the complex flows within them.

THE VALUE OF CHILD LABOUR

The opportunity cost of eliminating child labour is the value of this labour itself: to the children, to their households and to the larger community. Here is where controversies surrounding policy are joined. Those who would move more rapidly to oppose child labour see this cost as relatively manageable and dwarfed by the benefits of taking action. Those who would go slower believe these costs to be quite large; they stress that well-intended actions by child labour activists may actually hurt those they are trying to help. For some with a rational choice perspective, there is an initial presumption that the opportunity costs must be substantial, since parents (from this viewpoint) are often seen to choose to put their children to work. If parents are economically rational, and if they care about the future well-being of their children, they must be calculating that the benefits of child work exceed the costs of reduced opportunities for education.

An attempt to obtain the opportunity cost of eliminating child labour was made by the country study teams. In some cases, in which country teams had no household survey data, the wages of one or two occupations commonly held by children were used. In countries where there were available household survey data, the study teams used the children's monthly earnings, including salaries and payment in-kind, as the value of their work. The average monthly earnings were calculated for occupations related to domestic work, i.e., baby sitter, cleaner, cooker, cloth washer, etc.. When a child was reported to be doing domestic work and was not attending school, since there was no information on hours spent in household activities, researchers attributed a "domestic servant" salary earned by employed children. The earnings obtained by these methods were then pooled to determine the average opportunity cost of removing children from work.

We place great credence in the efforts of these study teams, whose methods are documented in their reports. Unfortunately, we have these detailed calculations for only a handful of countries. These could not be supplemented by data from labour force surveys, since, in general, these do not account for working children below the age of 14, and when they do, the work performed in the household and/or without monetary payment are seldom reported.

Because extrapolation from so few observations was not feasible, we chose to impute the value of child labour in most countries from the unskilled adult wage. The first step was to construct a series for the adult wage itself. We had direct observations for a few countries, primarily drawn from our study teams, but these too were insufficient for extrapolation. Instead, we relied on the ILO's LABORSTA database. These figures are reported by national governments are not vetted for accuracy; their precision is uncertain, but the general contours are plausible. We utilized the occupational series compiled by Freeman and Oostendorp (2000) and extracted the principal unskilled occupational categories to construct a composite unskilled wage for each of the 25 countries included in the LABORSTA sample. (The wages were converted to $PPP using conversion ratios for the years corresponding to the observations.) This core of observations was then extrapolated to the rest of the countries, as documented in Annex 2. Population-weighted mean unskilled wages estimated in this fashion are reported in Table 5.1.

Table 5.1. Mean annual unskilled adult wages by region, in $PPP

Region	Wage
Transitional countries	4 158
Asia and Pacific	2 386
Latin America	2 791
Sub-Saharan Africa	1 040
North Africa and Middle East	3 485
Global	**2 687**

Using the above adult wage estimates for countries for which we also have data on the value of child labour, we find that the unweighted mean of the ratio of child to unskilled adult wages is approximately 20%. This proportion is plausible, given that the younger age group, 6 to 11, comprise 43% of all working children (based on the medium estimate for the number of working 12 to 14 year-olds). Thus, we impute the value of child labour in each country as 20% of the adult wage, except for those countries for which we have direct observations on this variable. Since nearly all countries are estimated (only a few of our study countries provide direct measurements), the sensitivity of our measure of opportunity costs varies in approximately the same proportion as variations to this 20% ratio. That is, if the alternative ratio were 25% instead of 20%, the opportunity cost of child labour eliminated would rise by approximately one-fourth.

In estimating the value of child labour in this fashion, the study makes two important assumptions. First, it assumes that the remuneration, whether monetary or in kind, to children represents the value of their work. This may not be the case, however. Children may be overpaid as a disguised benefit to their parents from employers or other community members. They may be underpaid due to exploitation, a risk attributable to their susceptibility to adult authority. There is no way to determine which effect predominates a priori. Also, it assumes that the value of child labour foregone is not made up through the reallocation of unemployed adults to these same tasks, or that, if such reallocation occurs, it produces an equivalent loss in terms of other tasks abandoned. This assumption biases our estimates upward, since there are likely to be opportunities for substitution that mitigate the direct effects of withdrawing children from their work.

To complete the calculation of opportunity costs, each country's estimate of the value of child labour was multiplied by the number of working children from 5 to 14 years old. These results are reproduced in Table 5.2, which reports baseline totals for opportunity costs by wave.

Table 5.2. Baseline opportunity costs of child labour by wave, in $billion PPP

Region	Wave 1	Wave 2	Wave 3	Wave 4	Total
Transitional countries	2.0	3.0	4.4	6.7	16.0
Asia and Pacific	15.6	25.5	41.7	68.2	151.0
Latin America	3.1	5.1	8.5	14.1	30.9
Sub-Saharan Africa	2.5	4.5	8.2	14.8	30.1
North Africa and Middle East	1.8	3.1	5.2	8.7	18.8
Global	**25.0**	**41.2**	**68.0**	**112.6**	**246.8**

Since the total amount of child labour eliminated is approximately the same in each wave (subject to population growth or decline), the difference between these totals can be attributed primarily to discounting.

Here is an example at the level of a single country. Tanzania is estimated to have nearly two million child labourers. Their average opportunity cost is approximately $260 per child per year. Multiplying these two together yields $520 million. Since Tanzania's national income in 2000 was nearly $16.9 billion, the total economic contribution of this country's child workers (market and non-market) amounts to just over 3% of all market earnings.

DEFRAYING HOUSEHOLD OPPORTUNITY COSTS BY AN INCOME TRANSFER PROGRAMME

Underlying the perspective on education in this study is the assumption that there are three overriding factors that determine whether parents will choose to transfer their children from work to full-time school attendance. First, education of sufficient quality must be readily available to them. This has been addressed in the previous section on the supply side of education. Second, they must be able to overcome the purely economic barriers to having their children engaged in study. This includes the direct cost of schooling, such as fees and uniforms, but also, and especially, the opportunity cost, i.e. the value of the work children might have to give up if they increase their school participation. Third, even if they enjoy the physical and financial availability of education for their children, parents may choose not to have them take advantage of it for various cultural or social reasons.

In this section, we explore in more detail the second of these reasons; the third is addressed in Chapter 6.

School attendance is sometimes prohibitively expensive because of the fees imposed on parents, such as for books and uniforms. Even when school attendance is completely "free", however, its opportunity cost – the value of the work children perform when they are not in school – may be too great to bear. Increasingly, analysts of child labour are coming to the view that some form of monetary transfers to low-income parents may be necessary to defray the explicit and implicit costs of education.

The study envisions that some sort of income transfer programme will be adopted on a global basis. National governments will target eligible households, calculate specific amounts to be transferred to each, disburse the money and monitor the school attendance of children. Actually, in many countries, such programmes have been already launched, such as *Bolsa Escola* and the *Programa de Erradicação do Trabalho Infantil* (PETI) in Brazil, the *Programa de Educación, Salud y Alimentación* (PROGRESA) in Mexico, Food for Education (FFE) in Bangladesh, and others. See Box 5.1 for further details on two of these, *Bolsa Escola* and PETI.

To obtain the transfer expense of eliminating child labour, the country study teams determined the appropriate level of income below which households were classified as "poor", as well as the number of poor households with school age children. A hypothetical income transfer programme was then established that would provide poor families with a grant equal to 80% of the value of child labour times the number of school-age children, irrespective of whether their children were actually working, provided the sum does not exceed the average poverty gap (the average amount poor families would need to meet the poverty line). If it does, they receive an amount equal to the poverty gap, unless 60% of the value of child labour times the number of children still exceeds this amount, in which case they get the latter grant. We envision the programme being phased in over the 20-year study horizon; thus the stimulation of education demand through transfers takes place at roughly the same pace as the expansion of the quantity and quality of education.

Contrary to many government programmes that target working children in general or those in hazardous activities, we estimate a programme in which all poor children are eligible to receive transfers. We have three reasons for this. First, children tend to move in and out of the labour force more frequently than adults; so it would be hard to distinguish between "working" and "non-working" children (Levison et al., 2002). Second, even if we had longitudinal data that permitted a distinction of this sort, it would be prohibitively expensive to monitor it at the household level. Finally, existing surveys rarely account for household activities, which are among children's main tasks in developing countries.

Quite clearly, our hypothetical transfer programme is generous. We are guided by our mission to model the elimination of child labour and not

Box 5.1. Examples of income transfer programmes

The *Bolsa Escola* programme distributes income to families below the poverty line while requiring school-age children to attend class. Each child receives R$15 or US$12 (PPP) per month, but no more than three children per household can receive this financial assistance. This programme benefited more than 8.2 million children as of December 2001, amounting to almost US$1.2 billion (PPP) per year. This programme has existed since 1995, and although it does not directly address the issue of child labour, it does help to reduce its incidence through income received by the family, which substitutes for the children's earnings. The only requirement for eligibility is to have children of school age (6 to 15) and to have an income that is not above the poverty line, calculated by dividing the total money income (as a multiple of the monthly minimum salary) by the number of family members. In return, the family commits to the children's school attendance while receiving the benefit.

Another effective social programme implemented in Brazil is the Child Labour Eradication Programme (PETI), which is similar to *Bolsa Escola*, except that the money is given to poor families with school-age children (7 to 14 years old) engaged in the worst forms of labour, and it is conditioned on children going to school instead of working. The PETI programme started in 1996 in 13 counties in Mato Grosso do Sul state, where a significant number of children worked in coal mines, and it has since expanded to all states of Brazil. Children from counties above 250,000 inhabitants and from the state's capital receive US$32 PPP per month (R$40), while others receive US$20 PPP (R$25). In December 2001, 749,353 children benefited from this programme in Brazil, resulting in government expenditure of US$27.6 million (PPP) or US$330.9 million (PPP) per year, which equals a monthly value of US$36.80 (PPP) per child. In addition to the direct benefit given to each child, the programme also includes a supervised time of leisure, culture and sports, complementing children's school time. Moreover, orientation and support through social and educational activities are given to children's families. Currently, the industries targeted by the programme are: coal and other mining, brick manufacture, milling, joinery, trash collection, quarrying, textiles, salt processing, meat-packing, fishing, and plantation agriculture in cotton, tobacco, sugar-cane, citrus, sisal, etc..

The Education, Health and Nutrition Programme (PROGRESA) in Mexico started in August 1997 and targeted rural households living in extreme poverty. It now operates in almost 74,000 rural communities distributed across more than 2,000 counties in 31 states and benefits approximately 3.2 million households. Children below the age of 18 are provided with monetary grants if enrolled in school. In addition, a basic preventive health package is provided to family members free of charge, including a dietary supplement to undernourished pre-school children. PROGRESA accounts for less than 20% of the federal government budget allocated to poverty reduction.

The Food for Education programme (FFE) in Bangladesh began in July 1993 and relies on food transfer (rice and wheat) to the poor conditioned on school attendance. The programme was able to appreciably increase school attendance at a modest net cost to the current income of poor families. In 2000, the programme covered almost 18,000 primary schools and benefited about 2 million households.

merely its diminution. More modest and targeted programmes, like *Bolsa Escola* and PETI may also be more cost effective, but they fall short of the objectives of this study. We propose to limit reimbursement to a maximum of 80% of the value of child labour, on the other hand, because we expect that education will be seen as transmitting noticeable benefits to households, particularly in light of the quality improvement expenditures described in

Chapter 4. Even at 80% reimbursement (or less depending on the effect of the poverty gap), the transfer programme could be regarded as occupying the upper end of the policy spectrum: it is more likely to overstate than understate the necessary costs of meeting the study's education and child labour objectives.

In addition to the transfer of funds, we assumed unit administrative costs for the programme to be 5% of unit transfers. In principle, it is important to keep these two types of costs separate, since only the administrative costs are "real" resource costs in the economic sense. It is vitally important, from the standpoint of economic theory, to maintain the distinction between real resource expenditures, such as administrative costs, and income transfers. Redistributing money from some members of society to others is a financial cost to those from whom the money is taken, but it does not in itself represent a diminution of the productive resources of society.

Table 5.3 reports the baseline transfer expenditures (without administrative overhead) by wave:

Table 5.3. Total transfers by region and wave, in $billion PPP

Region	Wave 1	Wave 2	Wave 3	Wave 4	Total
Transitional countries	2.2	3.7	1.9	5.2	13.1
Asia and Pacific	21.6	35.7	18.3	50.2	125.8
Latin America	4.0	6.7	3.4	9.4	23.5
Sub-Saharan Africa	5.0	8.2	4.2	11.6	29.1
North Africa and Middle East	3.8	6.3	3.2	8.8	22.1
Total	**36.6**	**60.6**	**31.1**	**85.3**	**213.6**

By combining data on the value of child labour foregone and the transfer payments received by households, we can construct an estimate of the net short run effects of the study model on the household sector. This is reported in Table 5.4, recalling that the specific households experiencing the opportunity costs and receiving the payments are not necessarily the same.

Overall, transfers are slightly lower than the lost value of child labour, with modest variation between regions. The household sector experiences its sole gain in North Africa and the Middle East, where families are larger, and nearly breaks even in Africa for the same reason. In general, the slightly negative balance elsewhere can be regarded as acceptable. Since there is considerable economic advantage to schooling, full compensation should not be necessary to provide an incentive for parents to choose education over work for their children. Also, many child workers come from non-poor households, so the transfer programme most likely exceeds the opportunity cost of the poor households in particular.

Table 5.4. Opportunity costs and transfer payments within
the household sector by region, in $billion PPP

Region	Costs	Transfers	Net Position
Transitional countries	16.0	13.1	-2.9
Asia and Pacific	151.0	125.8	-25.2
Latin America	30.9	23.5	-7.4
Sub-Saharan Africa	30.1	29.1	-1.0
North Africa and Middle East	18.8	22.1	3.3
Total	**246.8**	**213.6**	**-33.2**

To conclude this chapter, we would like to consider the consequences of alterations in the assumptions made in the model and the process of data extrapolation. First, we can consider the impact of a decision to reimburse a maximum of 75% of the value of child labour, rather than 80%. This counterfactual is reported in Table 5.5:

Table 5.5. Sensitivity of transfer programme costs to a reduction
in maximum reimbursement rate, in $billion PPP

Region	Transfer at 80% Max.	Transfer at 75% Max.
Transitional countries	13.12	13.12
Asia and Pacific	125.79	125.78
Latin America	23.53	23.37
Sub-Saharan Africa	29.05	28.92
North Africa and Middle East	22.09	22.09
Total	**213.58**	**213.29**

Due to the role of the poverty gap in the transfer formula, the decrease in global transfers is negligible.

As was mentioned earlier in this chapter, there were insufficient data on the value of child labour to perform a valid extrapolation to the entire set of countries, and we simply assigned to most of them a value of child labour equal to 20% of the unskilled adult wage. Table 5.6 reports the sensitivity of the transfer calculation to an increase in this ratio to 25%.

Global transfers rise at a rate of approximately 21.5%, somewhat less than the percentage increase in the estimate of the value of child labour. Note that this higher transfer rate would be applied against an upward revision of opportunity costs.

Table 5.6. Sensitivity of transfer programme costs to changes in the assumed ratio of the value of child labour to the unskilled adult wage, in $billion PPP

Region	Total Transfer at 20% Ratio	Total Transfer at 25% Ratio
Transitional countries	13.12	16.19
Asia and Pacific	125.79	154.05
Latin America	23.53	26.51
Sub-Saharan Africa	29.05	35.18
North Africa and Middle East	22.09	27.57
Total	**213.58**	**259.49**

Taking these sensitivity exercises together, it is apparent that the opportunity cost and transfer totals are stable across a wide range of alternative assumptions. Fluctuations in the calculated amounts due to these factors would not substantially alter the basic relationships reported in Chapter 2.

PUBLIC SECTOR COSTS
OF ELIMINATING CHILD LABOUR

6

In Chapter 4, we considered the costs of expanding the quantity and quality of education to accommodate the influx of children withdrawn from child labour. In this chapter, we turn to the costs assumed by the public sector to directly reduce both demand and supply for child labour. On the supply side, the main intervention we envision is an income transfer programme that would defray the cost to households of removing their children from productive work. On the demand side (and also to some extent supply), we propose a diverse set of targeted activities that would reach children for whom the income transfer programme is not sufficient.

The first of these, the income transfer programme, has been analysed in the preceding chapter. It was pointed out there that income transfers, while placing a financial burden on governments, do not constitute true economic costs, since no goods or services are reallocated from other uses. This is fundamental to the economic perspective and characteristic of cost-benefit studies in particular. Nevertheless, such programmes need to be administered, and the labour and related resources devoted to this task *are* economic costs in the above sense. For this reason, we will briefly turn to administrative costs connected with implementing the income transfer.

We have uncovered little evidence that would point to a procedure for estimating these costs. Instead, we make the ad hoc assumption that 5% of the transfer would be required for administration. This is less than the rate for well-established income transfer programmes in the developed countries, but we recognize that it may be either to high or too low (or both across different regions). Thus, while 5% is used for baseline calculations, this figure can be raised or lowered by plausible amounts to gage the effect on net benefits as established in Chapter 2. Each 1% change is associated with approximately $2 billion in present value costs over the 20-year study horizon. This sum, however, does not appear large in the context of this study.

The second public sector cost, pertaining to intervention programmes, requires more analysis. The elimination of child labour, particularly in its worst forms, can only be a complex undertaking, involving changes in many dimensions of society. In practice, however, institutions pursuing this goal have to take background conditions as given and work within their constraints. The result has been a flow of programmes designed to combat specific instances of child labour through direct intervention. Such interventions can be supply-side, such as campaigns to dissuade children from working in particularly hazardous occupations, or demand-side, such as investment in increased surveillance and enforcement capacity to deter those who would exploit child labour. In either case, they attempt to achieve their objectives even though many of the underlying conditions that give rise to child labour persist.

This is also the approach taken in this study, since more far-reaching transformations are beyond its scope and, in any event, too little is known about the systemic forces that generate child labour overall and in its worst forms. Thus, the study envisions a replication of successful existing interventions up to the level needed to eliminate child labour. In order to generate the costs of these programmes, we needed to know three components: (a) the number of children targeted, (b) the appropriate mix of programmes, and (c) their unit costs.

a) The number of children targeted: It is assumed that, over time, *all* children in the worst forms of child labour will be prevented from future work of this sort by programme interventions. In addition, children whose work interferes with schooling – either prohibiting it altogether or interfering with its success – *may* be targeted for intervention if there are reasons to believe that income transfers, combined with the availability of quality schools, will not be enough to get the job done. We assumed that all children in the unconditional worst forms of child labour (see Chapter 3) fall into this category, as well as socially excluded children, such as children of the lowest caste in some countries, or refugee children. Moreover, since we envision the elimination of the worst forms of hazardous labour within the condensed time frame of ten years, children in hazardous activities might be targeted by special interventions beyond those related to education demand and supply. Nevertheless, we also considered that it might be unnecessary to encompass the entire target group through interventions, since there may be spillover effects (setting examples, bandwagon effects, a minimum number of children engaged required for the continuation of a particular form of child labour) that permit child labour to be curtailed even without 100% coverage.

b) The appropriate mix of programmes: The last decade has seen an enormous expansion of new programmes to combat child labour. In a spirit of learning from experience, many institutions have experimented with a wide variety of methods, some more successful, others less. Our study built on this experience in the following way: (1) It assumes that the most effective mix of interventions is likely to be country-specific. Rather than proposing a universal recipe, we followed the lead of those who have worked on the ground to develop these programmes. In other words, the actual country mix was the starting point for determining the putative effective country mix, incorporating only those interventions, or portions of interventions, that were concerned with the elimination of child labour in its various forms. For example, if a programme provides medical assistance to children performing hazardous work, it is not considered part of the mix necessary to eliminate such work. (2) It assumes that we can learn through trial and error to the extent of not repeating programmes that had weak results. In determining the mix and unit cost of interventions, we eliminated from the reference group (the set of interventions used for cost extrapolation in the study) those significantly above the median in unit costs. (3) It assumes that, drawing on successful experience and having access to an adequate supply of human talent, we can replicate past interventions at whatever scale is necessary. This last assumption permits direct extrapolation.

c) The unit cost of interventions: Calculating the unit cost of programme interventions is difficult, as there is no pre-existing literature from which we could have constructed benchmarks to be used at the country level. In each instance, numerator and denominator data had to be calculated directly from country experience.

- The *numerator* was the total cost of intervention, summed over the entire mix. We would have liked to distinguish start-up from recurrent costs, and use only the latter for calculating the cost totals for the out years of existing programmes. However, such information was not forthcoming in many countries. The costs included expenditures made by (or financed by) all actors, including all units and levels of government, all nongovernmental organizations and all external donors. Only those expenditures tied to the portions of programmes relevant to the elimination of child labour were counted.

- The *denominator* was the number of children withdrawn or prevented from engaging in child labour, as reported to us by the programme managers.

Using this approach, we assumed that the elimination of child labour, in general and in its worst forms, requires the replication of interventions so as to reach all target children directly or indirectly, and that the appropriate mix of interventions is given by the actual mix at the country level. Thus, we estimated the unit cost of a standard package of interventions and multiplied it by the number of children to be reached.[1]

---

[1] It is reasonable to expect that there will be increasing marginal unit costs of intervention to the extent that later programmes target the most resistant cases remaining after others have been resolved. We are unable to pursue this, since we had no data from which a marginal cost schedule could be derived. This introduces a modest downward bias to our estimates.

DATA SOURCES AND RESULTS

IPEC commissioned a review of Action Programmes to eliminate child labour. Based on a review of the IPEC Programme Database and several other documents, a questionnaire was developed and distributed to the IPEC Field Offices for selected Action Programmes. The questionnaire requested general information on the Action Programmes (implementing agencies, implementation period, major interventions etc.), information on the target group (age, gender, and nature of work) and cost information (start- up costs and operating costs broken down by sources of fund, allocation of total costs by major interventions, and grand total of costs).[2]

The survey yielded data collected from 77 ILO-IPEC Action Programmes in 18 countries, which were used as a basis for the regional extrapolation. While the reviewed Action Programmes included interventions targeted not only toward unconditional worst forms of child labour (many were in fact targeted toward hazardous work), we assumed that, on the whole, the unit costs would not differ significantly across different forms of child labour.[3]

Table 6.1 presents the costs of interventions for to withdraw and prevent children from the unconditional worst forms of child labour, according to low, medium and high estimates of the number of children as presented in Chapter 3. Unit costs are calculated on the basis of a case-weighted average, corresponding to the different case estimates – which is why they vary between low, medium and high estimates.

Unit costs are highest in Latin America. This can partly be explained by the fact that a high percentage of programmes in Latin America have targeted children in sexual exploitation. Such programmes are typically expensive due to the importance of one-on-one work and the necessity of rehabilitative measures. Regional differences also reflect the local costs of labour and other expenses. Note that, as larger numbers of worst forms estimates are incorporated, the weight of total costs shifts from Latin America to Asia. This in turn accounts for the decline in global unit costs (due to composition effects).

We can add socially excluded children on whom we had data (refugee children and *dalit* children in Nepal) to the target group of interventions. The number of children and the costs of interventions targeting them are presented in Table 6.2, applying the same unit costs as above.

It should be stressed that this table is based on a highly incomplete count of potentially socially excluded children. Presumably, millions of children are

---

[2] For a closer look at the results by country, form of child labour and type of intervention, see Ueda (2002).

[3] At least, this seems to be the case for forced and bonded labourers, who represent more than two thirds of the total of children in the unconditional worst forms, whereas the unit costs of removing children from sexual exploitation or trafficking may be higher.

Table 6.1. Costs of interventions to eliminate the unconditional worst forms of child labour, in $million PPP (unit costs in $PPP)

Region	Low estimate		Medium estimate		High estimate	
	Unit costs	Total costs	Unit costs	Total costs	Unit costs	Total costs
Transitional countries	637	6	637	6	637	6
Asia and Pacific	199	1 310	172	2 188	164	3 017
Latin America	1 615	1 432	1 623	1 545	1 629	1 658
Sub-Saharan Africa	306	211	300	231	296	252
North Africa and Middle East	139	19	139	19	139	19
Total	**359**	**2 978**	**274**	**3 989**	**242**	**4 951**

Table 6.2. Costs of interventions for socially excluded children, in $million PPP (number of children in 1'000)

Region	Number of children	Costs of interventions
Transitional countries	689	453
Asia and Pacific	1 222	344
Latin America	101	116
Sub-Saharan Africa	1 222	384
North Africa and Middle East	997	208
Total	**4 231**	**1 505**

stigmatised in some fashion that would complicate their withdrawal from child labour and full participation in school, but are not refugees or members of a low caste (in a single Asian country). On the other hand, it also assumes that 100% of such children must be targeted, at a marginal cost equal to those entailed in reaching just a small fraction at present. To the extent that there are spillover effects of interventions, it may be that extending intervention to a larger population will not be accompanied by a proportionate increase in costs.

As mentioned earlier in this chapter, in principle we expect that interventions will be directed toward not only children in unconditional worst forms of child labour or in social exclusion, but also many in hazardous occupations. Unfortunately, there are not sufficient data on this target population to permit extrapolation to national or even regional levels.[4] Nevertheless, in Table 6.3 we add the additional costs of programmes directed

---

[4] ILO (2002) reported only global, not regional, totals for hazardous work.

toward those children identified as working under hazardous conditions in the 13 countries utilized in ILO (2002). Note that this is an enumeration, in the sense that no attempt was made to extrapolate these cases to the rest of the world. We have chosen this approach to maintain consistency with the other worst forms treated in this chapter.

Table 6.3. Costs of interventions for children in hazardous occupations, in $million PPP (number of children in 1'000)

Region	Number of children	Costs of interventions
Transitional countries	–	–
Asia and Pacific	5 047	729
Latin America	4 587	9 882
Sub-Saharan Africa	731	212
North Africa and Middle East	408	62
Total	**10 774**	**10 885**

Despite the fragmentary nature of the evidence, it is almost certainly the case that hazardous work constitutes the majority of the worst forms of child labour. In fact, the ratio of the number of children reported in Table 6.3 to those in other worst forms likely understates the relative importance of hazardous work. On the other hand, taken in the context of the previous two tables, Table 6.3 should be viewed as giving too large a profile to the cost of removing children from dangerous work situations. One reason is that a large fraction of the observations come from Latin America, which also has a far higher unit cost of intervention. But this cost difference is largely due, as was pointed out earlier, to the concentration of interventions against prostitution in the programme mix. Since very few of the interventions directed against hazardous work are likely to address prostitution, this cost differential may be misleading. Also, and more generally, it is not clear that programmes will be required to target all children in hazardous work. Many of these will be removed from their situations in the course of eliminating child labour overall. On the other hand, at least some programmes will be required, either because the occupations in question are resistant to other approaches, or to rehabilitate children who have been harmed by this work, or in order to accelerate its elimination as a matter of priority. Thus, for the purposes of this study, we include hazardous work in the same manner as social exclusion and the unconditional worst forms.

In scrutinizing the programme cost data in this chapter, it is apparent how fragmentary our evidence is, a point to which we will return in Chapter 9. For now, it should be borne in mind that the combined costs to the public sector are significantly underestimated; they could well be several times those we calculate in this study. On the other hand, even if this uncertainty is taken into account, given the relatively limited weight of programme costs compared to other cost and benefit items, the general conclusions of the study – the pronounced surplus of costs over benefits and the approximate magnitude of funding flows needed to implement the model – remain intact.

THE BENEFITS OF EDUCATION

7

In the cost calculations for the supply side of education, we assumed that all children aged 6 to 14 who are out of school would be in school by 2020 and that the quality of the existing schools would be improved where necessary, decreasing the pupil to teacher ratio where necessary and establishing a minimum expenditure on books and other materials. This chapter attempts to calculate the benefits children out of school would obtain if their years of education were increased. Of course, there is also an economic gain to the individual who had his or her school's quality improved, which would ideally be taken into account. This is not feasible, however, both because our measures of quality are highly imprecise, and because there is little international evidence on the economic returns to quality. For these reasons the study adopts the simplified assumption that the benefits come only from increased years of education.

It is also an assumption of this study that many important benefits of the elimination of child labour, such as the enhanced opportunity for personal development and social inclusion, are resistant to economic quantification. As a result, no attempt will be made to account for them. Only the strictly economic benefits from more widespread education – greater income for the individual, more rapid economic growth for the society – will be estimated, and not the cultural and social benefits. As Chapter 2 stressed, in a technical sense, this is not a true cost-benefit analysis but a study of net economic costs (or benefits). It is not designed to tell us what decision to make, but to advise us of the economic costs and benefits of that decision.

There are two general ways economists have calculated the benefits of education, through earnings equations and macroeconomic growth accounting. A brief review of the techniques and results will be illuminating, since they point toward the complex problem of determining how the benefits are distributed.

To measure the benefit to an entire economy, we could use either a longitudinal, growth-accounting approach or a cross-sectional regression

Box 7.1. Earnings equations

The earnings approach attempts to measure the present value of increased lifetime income attributable to greater educational attainment. What we would like to know, according to this method, is, if an average individual acquires Y rather than X years of schooling (where $Y>X$), how much more is she likely to make over the course of her working life, discounted back to the present? We could then compare this amount to the cost of acquiring Y-X additional years (including of course the opportunity cost) to determine whether education as an investment enjoys a positive rate of return. To conduct such an analysis, we would need detailed information on a large number of individuals with different levels of education, including all the other factors that might affect their income, based on the assumption that past relationships will continue into the future.

The best method would be that of "full discounting", in which each specific year of education is analysed separately. After all, while sixth grade, twelfth grade, and the final year of a Ph.D. are all "one year of education", each is likely to have a different effect on an individual's earning profile. This approach is highly data-intensive however, since it seeks to determine a large number of values (the economic effects of all the specific years of education), rather than just one. As a result, economists have more often employed the less demanding "Mincerian" approach, which treats years of education as essentially interchangeable.* Differences in the marginal effect of an extra year's education are captured, if at all, by enabling curvature in the wage-education relationship – for instance, by introducing a term for the square of the years of education. The general form of a Mincerian wage equation is:

$$W_i = C + \beta^X_i X_i + \beta^E_i E_i$$

where C is a constant, W_i is the wage of the ith individual, X_i is a vector of wage-relevant personal characteristics for i, E_i is i's educational attainment, and the β's are regression coefficients that convey the contribution of E and X to W. In effect, the equation solves for the effects of education and other characteristics (age, experience, gender, etc.) on the distribution of wages. (Typically W is the natural logarithm of wages, so that the coefficients measure percentage effects.) Thus a Mincerian analysis provides an average of the greater or lesser effects that might be attributed to additional years of schooling at different grade levels. The main assumptions are that the effects of all variables are independent of one another, all relevant variables are included in the model, there are no measurement difficulties, and the structure of the model is correct (shape of the functions, role of the constant, etc.). Such a model is theoretically less precise, because it forces each year of education to play the same role, whether or not that is true in actuality.**

A troublesome question is whether causation runs from education to the individual or from the individual to the likelihood of education. Is an individual's higher wage attributable to greater schooling, or are more skilled or ambitious individuals more likely to attend school, so that differences in both schooling and income are due to these individual traits? A large literature has developed in which economists have attempted to disentangle these influences. Recent evidence in developed countries tends to support the view that apparent returns to schooling really are what they seem, and not a proxy for unmeasured individual differences (Ashenfelter and Rouse, 2000). On this issue, the Mincerian approach appears justified.

In the Mincerian model, β^E_i represents the percentage increase in individual i's wage attributable to an additional year of education. If we sum these amounts, evaluated at the average wage for the community, we would get the total individual wage effect of education. This is not necessarily the same as the economy-wide benefit, however, for reasons considered below.

* The name comes form Jakob Mincer, an economist who pioneered this technique; see Mincer (1974). ** There is another assumption embedded in the use of Mincerian, as well as economy-level, approaches to the economic benefits of education in a study such as this: that past benefits are a reliable guide to future ones (Bennell, 1996). Economic transformation in the course of development can alter these relationships. To some extent, the baseline nature of the current study, abstracting as it does from development, blunts the force of this critique. Nevertheless, achievement of universal primary and lower secondary attendance, as we envision, would be expected to alter past patterns. While this appears true, there is no means to correct for it, and so we can simply note it here.

similar to the Mincerian technique for individuals, only applied to countries. The first of these fits the historical data for a single country to an aggregate production function; by relating growth in output to growth in broad categories of inputs, the approach seeks to determine the extent of each input's contribution to output. The result – again, predicated on the assumption that the model captures the relevant variables in the correct way – provides us with a measure of education's contribution to economic growth. The advantage of this approach is that, being country-specific, it avoids attributing to education or other variables the effects of a country's unique historical and social dynamics. For this reason, the longitudinal method is often called a "fixed effects" approach. Also, by looking at changes within one country over time rather than many countries at a single moment in time, the approach avoids the necessity of imposing a one-size-fits-all model on countries that may be too diverse to model in the same way. The disadvantages with this approach are twofold: it is highly dependent on assumptions regarding the relationship between inputs and outputs in production, and, with many events taking place simultaneously over time, it is difficult to discern what is causing what. The cross-section method, by contrast, attempts to explain the variation in national economic growth rates (or static levels of income per capita) by differences in explanatory variables such as education. Given sufficient cross-national data sets, this type of analysis is easy to perform, but care is required to determine if the results reflect true causal effects or merely the spurious correlation of measured differences with unmeasured ones. For instance, if countries with more widespread education also have more effective economic institutions (not easy to measure), the explanatory power attributed to education may be misplaced.

The sum of individual benefits is not necessarily equal to the benefit of the entire society; in principle it could be either greater or less. It can be less, because education may have positive externalities. For example, a more educated worker may make his colleagues more productive as well, and a more educated populace can be the foundation for more effective political and economic institutions. If there are positive externalities, the macroeconomic benefits will exceed the sum of individual wage gains. On the other hand, it is possible that the macroeconomic benefit could be less. This is because educational *credentials* (not actual skills acquired through education) may give their possessors an inside track in the labour market, permitting them to get choice jobs in place of others with fewer qualifications. To the extent that moving to the front of the job queue in this way reflects differences in credentials and not actual skills, the gain of the more educated is the loss of the less educated. If the entire value of education were of this sort – which it certainly isn't – we would see positive individual gains to schooling but no macroeconomic benefit at all. The issue boils down to how large the credentialing effect actually is; some studies find that it accounts for as much as a quarter of the total individual benefit of education.[1] The net effect of these two factors, positive externalities and credentialism – would determine whether the macroeconomic impact of education is greater or less than the sum of its measured wage benefits. In an ideal procedure, we would subtract the individual benefits of education from the macroeconomic benefits; if the difference is positive, we would be measuring positive externalities, and negative otherwise.

Unfortunately, as Krueger and Lindahl (2001) painstakingly demonstrate, current attempts to estimate macroeconomic returns to education are not robust enough to set alongside the individual-level benefits. The parameters specifying return to education in growth accounting studies are wildly sensitive to specification choices, while cross-national regressions are beset by massive measurement error. (The quality of education and wage data for most countries is poor.) Little confidence can be placed in their results. Moreover, as these authors point out, the notion that society-wide returns to education can be isolated from other factors that affect economic growth is illusory: if the spillover effects of education operate through changes in technology and social institutions, what does it mean to hold these other factors constant in order to isolate the effect of education? The result of their study is essentially negative – that there is no reason to suppose that the social return to education is any greater or less than the sum of individual returns. Intuitively, we could imagine that a country that combines investment in education with complementary economic and institution-building policies would enjoy a large social return, but that in the absence of this coordinated effort spillover benefits from education would be more modest – perhaps sufficient to offset credentialing effects. If so, abstracting from the potential for coordinated policy would be in the spirit of this study, which does not address causes or consequences of socio-economic development other than child labour. Therefore, this study will measure the social returns to education by equating them with individual returns.

The value of the Mincerian coefficient used in the computations is based on Psacharopoulos' (1999) study, which compiles a large number of cross-sectional data from many different countries in the world, obtaining their wage returns to education. The actual number used is 0.11, an approximately mean among developing countries, meaning that workers would have 11% increase in earnings for each year increase in the level of education. In the benefits of education we considered that the 11% return to education would

---

[1] The treatment of credentialing in the economics literature has been clouded by a tendency to conflate it with the signaling/screening model of Michael Spence (1973). This is one potential explanation for credentialing, but the job competition model of Thurow (1975), further formalized by Knight (1979), is another. Evidence for any particular model is less compelling than evidence for credentialing effects in general, as proxied by the extra return to diploma years. Significant empirical studies pertaining to the US include Hungerford and Solon (1987), Heywood (1994) Jaeger and Page (1996) and Habermalz (2003). Developing country evidence can be found in Shabbir (1991) and Schady (2000).

affect the average unskilled worker's wage, since only up to a lower secondary school education is considered in the cost calculations, i.e., children that were out of school would study eight years and therefore would not have high skills to get very large wages. Of course we can here be underestimating the benefits if after those eight years children actually foresee the importance of education to their well-being and decide to continue studying.

Hence, for calculating the direct monetary benefits of increased education we used the total number of additional years of education to be received multiplied by the Mincerian coefficient times the average unskilled adult's wage. The present value of the total benefit was obtained assuming that each person would receive earnings during 40 years of his or her life commencing at age 15, i.e. for every additional year of education there will be 40 years of enhanced earnings. However, this work span is a conservative forecast if we consider that life expectancy is increasing and has reached more than 70 years in many developing countries, as indicated in Table 7.1. Since most such countries afford few public pension benefits, and very few unskilled workers possess private pensions that would allow them to stop working, they usually continue working as they age. In some countries children support their parents, but there is little evidence that this would reduce work life expectancy by a significant amount.

When calculating the benefits of education our assumption is that each individual, upon reaching the age of 15, becomes economically productive. In the narrowest sense, this would mean that all children, upon leaving school, enter the paid labour force and remain there until retirement. This narrow understanding of "economically productive" corresponds to the population on which estimates of the Mincerian coefficient are based. Of course, this is an extreme assumption, which would be difficult to justify. A less demanding view is that many adults are not in the paid labour force but remain productive in some other way. This would include, above all, a wide range of household activities that are seldom remunerated but which are essential for the production of essential goods and services, such as subsistence agriculture, cleaning, cooking, raising children, etc. Taking into account

Table 7.1. Average life expectancy at 15 by region

Region	Life Expectancy at 15, 2000 – 2005
Transitional countries	57.78
Asia and Pacific	56.41
Latin America	58.93
Sub-Saharan Africa	44.58
North Africa and Middle East	57.65

Source: UN World Population Prospects, 2000 Revision.

Table 7.2. Education benefits by region and wave, in $billion PPP

Region	Wave 1	Wave 2	Wave 3	Wave 4
Transitional countries	9.5	28.0	43.6	64.7
Asia and Pacific	150.4	531.8	964.3	1 660.7
Latin America	10.1	54.9	111.7	226.7
Sub-Saharan Africa	31.4	111.0	212.0	367.4
North Africa and Middle East	22.2	79.6	145.9	252.4
Total	**223.7**	**805.3**	**1 477.5**	**2 571.9**

Table 7.3. Primary education benefits by region and wave, in $billion PPP

Region	Wave 1	Wave 2	Wave 3	Wave 4
Transitional countries	9.5	20.9	28.2	31.5
Asia and Pacific	150.4	372.2	569.9	682.9
Latin America	10.1	25.2	38.5	45.8
Sub-Saharan Africa	31.4	84.9	141.7	177.0
North Africa and Middle East	22.2	56.1	87.0	104.7
Total	**223.7**	**559.3**	**865.3**	**1 041.9**

Table 7.4. Secondary education benefits by region and wave, in $billion PPP

Region	Wave 2	Wave 3	Wave 4
Transitional countries	7.2	15.4	33.2
Asia and Pacific	159.6	394.4	977.8
Latin America	29.7	73.2	180.8
Sub-Saharan Africa	26.1	70.3	190.4
North Africa and Middle East	23.5	58.9	147.8
Total	**246.0**	**612.2**	**1 530.0**

Table 7.5. Education benefits by region and alternative Mincerian coefficients, in $billion PPP

Region	5%	7%	9%
Transitional countries	66.3	92.8	119.3
Asia and Pacific	1 503.3	2 104.6	2 705.9
Latin America	183.4	256.7	330.0
Sub-Saharan Africa	328.1	459.3	590.5
North Africa and Middle East	227.3	318.3	409.2
Total	**2 308.4**	**3 231.7**	**4 155.0**

this broader conception of economic activity, our calculation of the education benefits implicitly assumes that the Mincerian coefficient measures increased productivity not only in the paid labour force, but also in unpaid tasks. There is no reason to assume that this is the case of course. Nevertheless, there is considerable evidence that household and other self-production activities benefit from higher levels of education, and so applying the same rate to both types of work may not be greatly off the mark.

With these caveats, consider Table 7.2, which reports the benefits of increased education by five-year wave.

Note that the benefits are cumulative: in the first wave, a third of the primary-age children not initially in school begin to attend. Then in the second wave an additional third are brought in, but the first third remain continuing beneficiaries. This explains why there are rapidly rising totals from one wave to the next, despite the countervailing effects of discounting.

The distribution of benefits is clarified further by distinguishing between primary and secondary education, as indicated by Tables 7.3 and 7.4.

Several points need to be mentioned. First, Table 7.4 reports only three waves, since the model assumes that no expansion of lower secondary attendance will take place during the first wave. Second, the totals for lower secondary are much larger than for primary due to the much greater attendance gap to be made up during those grades. Third, the above results should not be interpreted as providing evidence for the relative merits of devoting resources to these two levels of education, because the methodology (based on the Mincerian coefficient) assumes equal returns to both for a given year of additional schooling.

Most of the inputs into the calculation of the education benefits are also inputs into the calculation of costs, so the ratio of the two will not be altered by adjustments for measurement error. The principal exception is the Mincerian coefficient itself. For purposes of comparison, Table 7.5 reports the totals by region for three alternative values of the coefficient, 5%, 7% and 9%.

Of course, given the formula employed, the education benefits are strictly proportional to the coefficient used to value each year of additional schooling. Nevertheless, it is interesting to note that, even under the most pessimistic forecast of the effect of education on future earnings, the benefits far exceed the costs. Indeed, this would remain the case if we were to further scale down the benefits by a further third or even a half, under the presumption that no economic gains accrue to adults who are outside the paid labour force.

The conclusion of this chapter is that households can expect to benefit substantially from the redirection of children from work to education. They may require an income transfer programme to assist them in this, but the financial costs of such a programme (which are not economic costs in the technical sense) are also substantially less than the prospective benefits.

HEALTH BENEFITS

8

This study breaks new ground by attempting to put an economic value on the health improvements associated with eliminating the worst forms of child labour. In doing this, we are following a recent pattern in research on international social policy: considering the linkages between social conditions and economic growth and development. There are good reasons for this trend. While it has long been known that economic development has important implications for social conditions, we are now recognizing that the arrow of causation runs in the other direction as well: health and education in particular are important determinants of economic success at the national level. In addition, countries have limited economic resources to devote to improving social conditions, and it is helpful to know the extent to which they may expect to find these offset by future economic gains.

The field of health has seen a tremendous growth of interest in economic aspects. Much of this has been spearheaded by the World Health Organization's (WHO) Commission on Macroeconomics and Health. By documenting the economic impact of preventable disease, WHO has mobilized global interest in public health initiatives. This has been reflected in proposals to alleviate the burden of HIV/AIDS in sub-Saharan Africa, link public health expenditures to external debt relief and create a global fund to combat tropical diseases like malaria. In addition, during the last decade, developed countries have sponsored research designed to estimate the economic impact of injuries and illnesses suffered at work. We will survey some of these studies in this chapter and relate them to our own attempt to identify the economic aspects of the worst forms of child labour.

In Chapter 3 we considered the available evidence for the prevalence of worst forms of child labour. Some of these, such as hazardous work and prostitution, are directly health-related, while others, such as bonded labour or illicit activities are not. The global elimination of child labour envisioned in this study entails the elimination of all worst forms as a priority within the first ten years. In doing so, we propose to eliminate the great majority of all negative health effects. (It is possible that some child work, when it entails suitable hours and activities, may even generate positive health effects. Under the guidelines of our model, based on the relevant ILO conventions, this work would continue.) Unfortunately, it is difficult to put a precise number on the health impacts we might expect to alleviate.

First, the linkage between worst forms of child labour and health outcomes is complex. Exposures due to improper work may have long-run consequences well into adult life, but no longitudinal studies have been conducted to generate this information. Simple comparisons between the health status of former child workers and those who did not work as children are not helpful due to the "healthy worker" effect: the tendency for the most healthy individuals to be placed in difficult and dangerous work situations. Thus, it may appear as though having been a child labourer is beneficial to future health, when it is actually healthy characteristics that cause both adult health and the greater likelihood of having worked as a child.

Second, epidemiological data on the health consequences of work are insufficient for both children and adults. We have reasonable data in the developed countries on industrial accidents, but not on industrial diseases, many of which have long latent phases and are subject to multiple causation. We have virtually no reliable data on occupational injuries in the developing world. In other words, we know little about children's occupational risks because we know little about occupational risks in general (Dorman, 2000). Even in the developed countries, where adult risks are relatively well-studied, far less research focuses on the risks facing children (Dorman, 2001). Such data as exist focus primarily on injuries, yet one ILO country survey found illnesses to be somewhat more common (ILO, 1998).

Third, to the extent that the reduction in child labour is accompanied by an increase in education, we may expect to see future improvements in health. More educated individuals enjoy better health, even controlling for economic status, and as parents they are more successful at providing for the health of their children. We have case study evidence for these effects, but not yet the sort of data that could be used in a global cost-benefit study.

Nevertheless, the health benefits of the elimination of child labour are too important to overlook. As we have seen, millions of children perform work that damages their current and future well-being, and researchers are increasingly aware of the role that public health plays in economic development. Moreover, the model embodied in this study posits an accelerated elimination of the worst forms of child labour, and, in the absence of a quantified health benefit, our focus on the goals of ILO Convention No. 182 would add only to the cost totals. Hence it was decided to generate measures of the health consequences of the worst forms and of the economic effects to which they might give rise.

An immediate practical difficulty is that health impairments take a great variety of forms, from the minor and transient to permanently disabling or even fatal. For the purposes of this study, the Disability-Adjusted Life Year, or DALY, developed by the WHO, serves as a convenient index.

Each type of impairment is rated according to its effect on an individual's functioning. Immediate death would represent the maximum number of DALYs, calculated as one DALY for each year of remaining life expectancy at the victim's age. Lesser impairments are calculated as fractions of a DALY (based on the percentage of function lost) and multiplied by the number of years (which may also be less than one) the impairment is expected to persist.[1] The main justification for employing DALYs in this study is that we are interested only in the economic aspects of injury and illness and not in the other human dimensions; therefore a measure of lost function is appropriate.

The second step was to estimate the number of DALYs attributable to inappropriate child labour. This task was complicated by the general lack of information on the health consequences of child labour, of course. Drawing on the work of Fassa (2003), we applied DALY methodology to the health impairments reported for working children in the United States. The frequency of each major type of injury by one-digit industry was converted into a unit expected DALY, on the basis of the number of children (full-time equivalent) employed in that industry and the DALY conversion by specific impairment. Thus Table 8.1 was constructed:

To apply this to country data, we utilized the composition of the child labour force. That is, for a given country, we first calculated the number of full-time equivalent (FTE) child workers in each industry by multiplying the actual number of working children by the ratio of average annual hours to 2000:

$$\text{FTE workers} = (\text{total number of workers}) \times (\text{average hours per week})$$
$$\times (\text{average weeks per year}) \div 2000$$

This calculation was performed separately for 5 to 14 and 15 to 17 year-olds and for each major industry. We then multiplied the number of FTEs (in hundreds) by the corresponding DALY coefficient from column four of Table 8.1. Summing over all industries and age groups, this gave us a total DALY estimate for the country. We had detailed employment data of this sort for 20 countries, derived from household surveys, and we used these observations to impute estimates for the rest of the world. Total DALYs associated with the worst forms of child labour are distributed by region as in Table 8.2.

It is clear that there are several biases built into this procedure. **(1)** Using US data biases our results downward, since it is likely that child work is safer in the developed countries, even after controlling for composition by major industry. **(2)** Using only injury data introduces a further downward bias, since illnesses are excluded completely. **(3)** Using all reported injuries for working children biases our results upward, since some

---

[1] For further details on the construction of the DALY index, see WHO (2002).

Table 8.1. Expected DALYs per 100 FTE child workers by major industry (US data)

	YLL per 100 FTE workers per year	YLD per 100 FTE workers per year	DALY per 100 FTE workers per year
Agriculture			
5 to 14 year-olds	0.74397	0.770908	1.514878
15 to 17 year-olds	0.68693	0.759466	1.446396
Mining			
5 to 14 year-olds	1.19904	1.470104	2.669144
15 to 17 year-olds	1.16760	1.448284	2.615884
Construction			
5 to 14 year-olds	0.56205	0.825893	1.387943
15 to 17 year-olds	0.55200	0.813394	1.365394
Manufacturing			
5 to 14 year-olds	0.14988	0.271402	0.421282
15 to 17 year-olds	0.14720	0.276644	0.423844
Service			
5 to 14 year-olds	0.11241	0.151844	0.264254
15 to 17 year-olds	0.11040	0.158149	0.268549
Retail			
5 to 14 year-olds	0.11241	0.364978	0.477388
15 to 17 year-olds	0.11040	0.378888	0.489288

YLL = Years of life lost due to premature mortality   YLD = Years lost due to disability

Source: Fassa (2003)

Table 8.2. Disability-adjusted life years due to worst forms of child labour by region

Region	Total DALYs
Transitional countries	192 710
Asia and Pacific	1 492 618
Latin America	206 897
Sub-Saharan Africa	730 562
North Africa and Middle East	274 100
Global	**2 896 887**

portion is attributable to work not in violation of Convention No. 182. Taking all three into account, it is likely that our calculation significantly underrepresents the true health costs of unsuitable child work. To the extent that this effect is constant across the countries in our sample, the impact can be assessed by simply scaling up our reported health costs by the corresponding hypothetical ratio of actual to reported DALYs.

The next step is to convert these DALY estimates into monetary impacts. Here it is important to be very clear. This study does not take the position that health outcomes can be reduced to monetary equivalents. The most important aspects of human health cannot be captured in economic measurements: they include the pain or discomfort of the individual suffering the impairment, the emotional burden on family members and the disruption to the many activities of daily life outside the economic sphere. We make no effort to incorporate them into our study. Nevertheless, ill health also has an economic dimension: work is performed more poorly or not at all, and there are disruptions to co-workers as well as disincentives to the accumulation of human capital. We would be missing a significant economic aspect of child labour if we did not make an attempt to measure and incorporate these effects. To put it differently, the economic costs of ill health due to the worst forms of child labour represent the economic component of a problem that is much more than economic.

The strategy for translating DALYs in monetary units can be described as follows. First, we surveyed the literature on the macroeconomic impacts of specific health stressors for estimations of economic outcomes. These are usually expressed as percentages of national or regional income. Second, we searched for estimates of the total number of DALYs associated with these stressors; this gave us economic cost per DALY. We then expressed this as a percentage of the average per capita income in the region under study, calculating this from the population-weighted average of national income per capita. Third, we applied this percentage to all the countries in our sample, using their values for worst form DALYs and income per capita. The result is the health cost estimate reported in our summary in Chapter 2.

Three health stressors of this sort appear in the literature: HIV/AIDS, occupational risk (from all sources) and malaria. While many studies have estimated the economic impact of HIV/AIDS, we were unable to obtain corresponding DALY estimates; hence this was not employed as a basis for imputing health costs.[2] Research on several countries, all in the developed world, has attempted to calculate the economic costs of occupational injuries and diseases; for a summary discussion, see Dorman (2000). The figure of 3% of GDP is typical, and this is also the overall number arrived at by the most meticulous study, that of Leigh et al. (1996). Using their result for the US as a benchmark, and taking the corresponding DALY estimates from WHO (2003), we arrived at 4.24 times per capita income as the cost per DALY.[3] This represents the upper boundary of our cost estimate.

---

[2] Economic impacts are estimated at the country level, whereas WHO reports DALY estimates only at the regional level.

[3] There are two caveats: (1) Since WHO reports DALYs for a North American region including Cuba and Canada, we extended the Leigh result to the entire region, using the regional average for per capita income as well. (2) The Leigh et al. study goes to great lengths to incorporate estimates of occupational disease, whereas these are largely missing from the WHO DALY estimates; hence the ratio of economic impacts to DALYs is biased upwards.

Due to the initiative of WHO, malaria, particularly in sub-Saharan Africa, has received considerable attention. We found three studies that provide plausible estimates of the economic impact of malaria in this region, McCarthy et al. (1999), Bonnel (2000) and Gallup and Sachs (2000). Using their estimates of aggregate economic impact, along with WHO data on DALYs and World Bank data on incomes, we arrive at percentages of per capita income per DALY of 3.6, 4.2 and 37.4 respectively. All of these DALY calculations are summarized in Table 8.3.

Table 8.3. Proportion of per capita income lost per DALY in four studies

Study	Leigh et al. (1996)	McCarthy et al. (1999)	Bonnel (2000)	Gallup and Sachs (2000)
Stressor	Occupational safety and health	Malaria	Malaria	Malaria
Region	North America	Sub-Saharan Africa	Sub-Saharan Africa	Sub-Saharan Africa
Total economic cost ($billion at PPP)	314.1	2.1	4.8	21.4
Total DALYs (billions)	**46.0**	**35.7**	**35.7**	**35.7**
Per capita income ($PPP)	32 199	1 600	1 600	1 600
Per capita income per DALY	4.243	0.036	0.042	0.374

Several aspects of this table are striking. The estimated loss of per capita income per DALY varies by a factor of approximately 100, more than one might expect. The higher North American result can be attributed to the high cost of medical treatment and the direct relationship to production. The malaria estimates, while lower, differ among themselves for technical reasons beyond the scope of this study. From the standpoint of the current analysis, it is likely that the most appropriate translation from health to economic impacts lies well between the extremes. The effects we are looking for are in developing countries, which do not generally share the highly institutionalized medical services of the United States and Canada. On the other hand, the health costs of the worst forms of child labour are exactly the sort of occupational injuries and illnesses that Leigh et al. were tabulating and should enter into the economy more directly than malaria. On yet another hand, however, the Leigh et al. results are biased upwards, from our perspective, by the fact that they pertain almost entirely to adults, whose wages and productivity are substantially higher than those of children (see Chapter 7).[4]

---

[4] Because they occur at younger ages, fatal and permanent non-fatal impairments to children will be associated with more DALYs, but not more economic impact per DALY. The difference in time structure between adult and child DALYs will be taken up in Chapter 9.

Table 8.4 demonstrates the sensitivity of our measure of health benefits to these different DALY–per capita income conversion rates.
In choosing between such disparate estimates, we should bear in mind their intuitive implications. At the high end, the Leigh et al. study implies that each DALY generates an ultimate economic cost over four times the average per capita income; at the low end, McCarthy et al., one full life year lost generates a cost of only 3.6% of per capita income. For our purposes, we judge the first too large and the second too small. Consider the case of a child who dies as a result of a worst form exposure. This will generate a stream of DALYs, beginning with an initial year in the current period and a series of additional years, each discounted to present value. The economic cost of the first year may be approximately equal to the child's productivity, which we estimate to be approximately 20% of an unskilled adult's. If the child's labour can be replaced without imposing a cost elsewhere in the economy, the immediate impact may be less; if there are disruptive effects that extend beyond the individual child, the impact may be greater. Future lost years are reduced in value due to discounting, but may be of greater future value, since they represent adult productivity. There are other considerations, however. Children who suffer debilitating but nonfatal injuries or diseases may require care which imposes significant burdens on family members, and a pattern of frequent and serious child disabilities can interfere with the accumulation of human capital.

With these considerations in mind, we judge that the intermediate result of Gallup and Sachs is, of the four, the most plausible, and we therefore employ it for our baseline estimates. It is likely that, as societies develop, and as medical care absorbs a higher fraction of national income and as education assumes a larger role in support of productivity, the share of per capita income represented by a DALY is likely to rise; hence the assumption that this relationship is fixed over the 20-year study period is conservative. Since calculated health costs are proportional to the DALY/economic conversion factor, the effects of hypothetical adjustments to this factor are straightforward.

Table 8.4. Health benefits (in $billion PPP)
by DALY–income per capita conversion rates

Study	Leigh et al. (1996)	McCarthy et al. (1999)	Bonnel (2000)	Gallup and Sachs (2000)
Transitional countries	45.1	0.4	0.4	4.0
Asia and Pacific	159.1	1.4	1.6	14.0
Latin America	43.7	0.4	0.4	3.8
Sub-Saharan Africa	24.6	0.2	0.2	2.2
North Africa and Middle East	44.7	0.4	0.4	3.9
Global	**317.2**	**2.7**	**3.1**	**28.0**

It is useful to compare the health benefits of eliminating the worst forms to the programme costs discussed in Chapter 6. Once again, we stress that the desirability of taking this action does not depend in any way on the comparison between economic costs and benefits, since the non-economic aspects of this problem carry enormous moral weight. Nevertheless, we can see that programme costs, to the extent they succeed in eliminating this enormous health burden, may well pay their own way, depending on the degree of undercounting of the worst forms target population examined in Chapter 3. As with other aspects of the child labour elimination model, however, the costs accrue more rapidly than the benefits. This time discrepancy plays an important role in the flow analysis of Chapter 9.

CONCLUSION: IMPLICATIONS FOR POLICY AND FUTURE RESEARCH

9

In Chapter 2, we provided the main result of the study, that there are substantial net economic benefits to the global elimination of child labour and its replacement by universal primary and lower secondary education. In the subsequent chapters we examined the individual cost and benefit components in greater detail, demonstrating their degree of plausibility and indicating the likely range within which alternative calculations would fall if the underlying assumptions were modified. We found that the baseline results are robust to these adjustments.

In this chapter we will consider two sets of implications for future efforts in the field of child labour elimination. First we will take a closer look at the financial feasibility of implementing the study model; then we will call attention to the most pressing data gaps revealed by this exercise.

FROM PRESENT VALUE TO FLOW ANALYSIS

The main results of the study were presented in Chapter 2 in the form of present values: the stream of costs and benefits were discounted back to their values in 2000. While this is appropriate for the purposes of comparing costs and benefits, it sheds little light on the issue of practicability. Means must be found to finance costs in each year, and the expectation of benefits in the future is no guarantee that this can be achieved. In this chapter we will convert the baseline results to year-by-year flows, so that practicability can be assessed.

In doing this, we are not altering the fundamental methodology of the study. The formulas for calculating costs and benefits remain exactly the same, except that, instead of generating future flows discounted back to present value (and reported in five-year waves), we generate 20 yearly flows without discounting. This permits us to identify the financial gaps (excesses

Table 9.1. Undiscounted yearly net benefits (costs) of the baseline model, in $billion PPP

| Programme year | Region | | | | | Global |
	Transitional countries	Asia	Latin America	Sub-Saharan Africa	North Africa and Middle East	
1	-0.8	-9.3	-1.2	-2.3	-1.2	-14.7
2	-0.8	-10.2	-1.3	-2.5	-1.3	-16.2
3	-0.8	-11.3	-1.5	-2.8	-1.4	-17.8
4	-0.8	-12.5	-1.7	-3.1	-1.6	-19.6
5	-0.9	-13.9	-1.9	-3.5	-1.8	-21.9
6	-1.3	-23.0	-3.5	-6.3	-2.8	-36.9
7	-1.2	-23.4	-3.8	-6.6	-2.7	-37.6
8	-1.2	-22.9	-3.7	-6.8	-2.7	-37.3
9	-1.0	-20.5	-3.7	-7.0	-3.0	-35.1
10	-0.9	-19.0	-3.6	-7.1	-2.8	-33.5
11	-0.7	-17.1	-3.5	-7.2	-2.5	-31.1
12	-0.6	-15.1	-3.3	-7.4	-2.0	-28.5
13	-0.5	-12.6	-3.2	-7.6	-1.7	-25.6
14	-0.4	-9.6	-3.0	-7.8	-1.2	-21.9
15	-0.2	-3.4	-2.7	-7.8	-0.6	-14.7
16	0.2	8.1	-1.8	-4.6	0.8	2.6
17	0.6	19.7	-0.8	-2.5	1.8	18.8
18	1.1	34.0	0.2	0.1	3.2	38.6
19	1.7	51.8	1.6	3.4	4.7	63.2
20	2.4	72.6	3.8	7.6	6.6	93.0

Figure 9.1. Undiscounted annual net financial benefits (costs), in $billion PPP

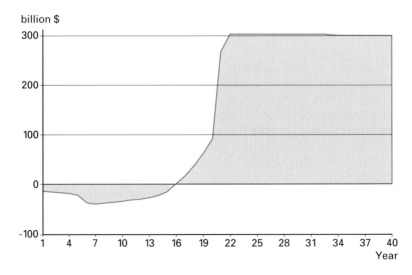

of economic costs over benefits) in future time periods, and to compare the burdens they impose to other flows in the global economy.

One particular difficulty with this time decomposition is that it requires assumptions about the distribution of DALYs between immediate and de-layed effects. In the present value wave calculation, all future impacts of DALYs were incorporated into the period in which impairment occurred. In the flow analysis, we must apportion these impacts into the years in which they are felt, not from which they originate. Of course, each type of injury or disease will have its own characteristic time profile, and the aggregate DALYs of each country will reflect different compositions of injuries and diseases. Because a more precise analysis is not possible, we made ad hoc assumptions about the flow of health costs over time. We assumed that 25% of the DALY would occur in the year of the trigger event, with 3% incre-ments accruing in each succeeding year.[1] The calculation of education ben-efits was more straightforward: we assumed that benefits would commence six years after the completion of an additional year of primary school and three years after a year of lower secondary school. Only benefits accruing during the 20-year period were counted; the flow analysis does not incor-porate the decades of continuing benefits after 2020.

Table 9.1 consolidates the cost and benefit items into yearly flows in this manner. It does not include the income transfer payments, but it does include the costs of administering the transfer programme. It also assumes that the benefits of primary education begin to accrue six years after the additional schooling takes place, whereas the delay is only three years in the case of lower secondary education.

This table vividly portrays the fundamental pattern in our economic flows: they are negative at the outset of the model, attain negative peaks in the middle of the first decade, turn positive up to a decade after this, and con-tinue to become more strongly positive as time elapses. This pattern is gov-erned above all by the front-loaded expenses of supplying and the back-loaded benefits of receiving additional education. Regions vary in their timing on the basis of the ratio of primary to lower secondary expansion. Transitional, Asian, North African and Middle Eastern countries achieve positive net flows first, 16 years into the programme, followed by the other regions two years later. Globally, negative net flows peak in year 7 at over $37.6 billion and turn positive by year 16. The global results are displayed graphically in Figure 9.1.

Here we can see the length of time required for the flows to turn pos-itive, and the enormous difference between the magnitudes of the initial net costs and subsequent net benefits.

The main point of the flow analysis is this: there is a lag of approxi-mately fifteen years between the inception of the child labour elimination programme and the beginning of net economic payoffs. This should not be

---

[1] Since only the first twenty years of costs and benefits are being modelled, there is little risk of overcounting DALYs. Indeed, there is greater risk of undercounting them.

Table 9.2. Annual fiscal impacts of child labour elimination, in $billion PPP

Programme year	Region					Global
	Transitional countries	Asia	Latin America	Sub-Saharan Africa	North Africa and Middle East	
1	0.8	10.3	1.4	2.7	1.5	16.6
2	1.2	14.3	2.1	3.7	2.2	23.4
3	1.5	18.4	2.8	4.7	2.9	30.2
4	1.8	22.6	3.5	5.7	3.6	37.1
5	2.2	26.8	4.2	6.8	4.3	44.3
6	2.8	38.8	6.4	10.2	5.9	64.2
7	3.2	43.4	7.2	11.5	6.6	71.9
8	3.6	47.9	8.0	12.8	7.4	79.7
9	3.8	51.2	8.8	14.1	8.8	86.8
10	4.2	56.0	9.7	15.6	9.4	94.9
11	4.5	61.0	10.3	17.1	10.0	102.9
12	4.9	66.4	11.2	18.8	10.4	111.8
13	5.3	72.3	12.2	20.7	11.0	121.6
14	5.7	78.7	13.1	22.9	11.5	132.0
15	6.1	83.2	14.2	25.1	12.1	140.7
16	6.4	84.0	14.8	24.5	12.0	141.6
17	6.7	86.5	15.5	25.3	12.3	146.3
18	7.0	88.6	16.3	26.1	12.5	150.5
19	7.2	89.9	17.2	27.0	12.7	153.9
20	7.4	91.6	17.4	27.6	12.9	156.9

Figure 9.2. Global fiscal impact of child labour elimination, in $billion PPP

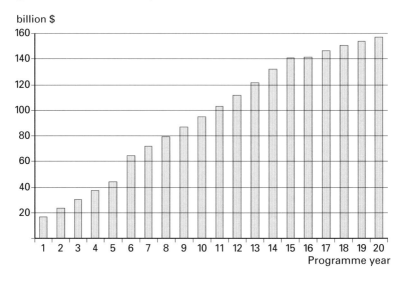

surprising given that the costs and benefits are both dominated by investments in education.

Perhaps the main practical concern is arranging the financing of the
programme. Here we are concerned with the public sector, which is re-
sponsible for implementing it. To isolate the fiscal impacts, we sum up the
costs of education, targeted interventions and the transfer programme, including the transfer payments themselves as well as administration costs.
From this, we deduct 20% of the benefit flows, under the assumption that
this proportion will be captured by the public sector in the form of increased
revenues. Excluded are opportunity costs and the remaining 80% of benefits, since they do not accrue to the public sector. The result over twenty
years is presented by region in Table 9.2 and globally in Figure 9.2.

The fiscal burden in Asia comprises more than half the total. Globally, the burden increases monotonically throughout the period, although
the rate of increase falls off during the final years when revenue gains begin
to be noticed. The average annual burden during the first decade is $54.9
billion; during the second it is $135.8 billion.

Table 9.3. Annual fiscal impacts of child labour elimination,
net of primary education, in $billion PPP

Programme year	Region					
	Transitional countries	Asia	Latin America	Sub-Saharan Africa	North Africa and Middle East	Global
1	-0.4	-3.9	-0.9	-0.9	-0.7	-6.9
2	-0.8	-7.6	-1.6	-1.8	-1.4	-13.1
3	-1.2	-11.2	-2.2	-2.6	-2.0	-19.3
4	-1.6	-14.9	-2.9	-3.4	-2.7	-25.5
5	-1.9	-18.5	-3.6	-4.3	-3.3	-31.7
6	-2.6	-29.8	-5.7	-7.5	-4.8	-50.4
7	-3.0	-33.7	-6.5	-8.4	-5.4	-57.1
8	-3.4	-37.6	-7.2	-9.4	-6.1	-63.7
9	-3.6	-41.4	-8.0	-10.4	-7.3	-70.6
10	-3.9	-45.3	-8.7	-11.3	-7.9	-77.1
11	-4.3	-48.9	-9.3	-12.3	-8.4	-83.2
12	-4.6	-52.9	-10.1	-13.3	-9.1	-90.0
13	-5.0	-56.9	-10.8	-14.4	-9.7	-96.8
14	-5.4	-60.9	-11.7	-15.5	-10.3	-103.8
15	-5.7	-63.9	-12.5	-16.6	-11.0	-110.0
16	-6.1	-68.2	-13.4	-17.8	-11.5	-117.0
17	-6.5	-72.6	-14.2	-19.1	-12.2	-124.6
18	-6.8	-76.9	-15.2	-20.5	-12.7	-132.2
19	-7.2	-80.9	-16.2	-22.0	-13.4	-139.7
20	-7.6	-85.8	-16.7	-23.5	-14.1	-147.7

Earlier it was pointed out that the child labour elimination programme we model expands on an existing commitment to universal primary education. It is therefore reasonable to ask what *additional* costs are entailed by our extending this commitment to achieve the more ambitious goals of universal lower secondary education and adherence to ILO Conventions Nos. 138 and 182. To calculate this, we eliminate the fiscal costs and revenues associated with primary education from Table 9.2; the results are in Table 9.3.

Comparing the final columns of Tables 9.2 and 9.3, we find that eliminating the fiscal role of universal primary education reduces the cost of financing the first year of the programme by approximately $9.8 billion. This difference between the total and incremental impacts increases from year to year, reaching its peak in 2015, when it reaches nearly $31 billion, 22% of the corresponding total impact. After this, the difference falls, as capital costs for primary education end and additional benefits associated with increased years of primary schooling accumulate. By the end of the programme period, the difference is just under $9.3 billion. Thus the effect of presenting child labour elimination as an "add-on" to the existing Millennium Development Goal in education is to reduce its fiscal burden substantially, although the bulk of the costs (and a smaller portion of the revenue) remain.

PUTTING THE RESULTS INTO PERSPECTIVE

The sums appearing in Table 9.2 are meaningful only in the context of the resources employed for other purposes. Table 9.4 provides four points of comparison. The first three are national public expenditures, the fourth an international financial flow.[2]

The simplest way to approach the issue of feasibility is to compare the two averages of annual fiscal impact at the global level (corresponding to the two decades of the programme) with the bottom row of Table 9.2, as in Figure 9.3 below. Recall that this approach considers only the fiscal impact; it does not take into account the full range of economic costs and benefits.

If the programme were perceived as an extension of the education budget (which, bearing in mind the great proportion of education to total expenditures, it largely is), and if education spending were carried forward without change until 2020, the child labour elimination programme during the first

---

[2] Expenditures were reported as shares of income. UNDP data were available for 1997-99 only and were converted based on 2000 GNI. For missing observations, expenditures were imputed using an unweighted regional average. For debt service, such imputations were not performed for oil-producing countries, where data was not reported. Also, it may be noted that our totals for education spending exceed those reported elsewhere, e.g. Delamonica et al. (2001). The difference can be explained by our use of PPP conversions for GNI, whereas the UNICEF authors convert GNI at market exchange rates.

Table 9.4. Payments in 2000 on education, health, military,
and debt service, in $billion PPP

Region	Education	Health	Military	Debt service
Transitional countries	116.6	108.8	70.7	132.3
Asia and Pacific	314.4	192.9	241.0	444.6
Latin America	161.6	120.9	46.6	286.5
Sub-Saharan Africa	59.3	25.8	24.2	44.6
North Africa and Middle East	92.9	44.1	110.9	100.8
Total	**744.8**	**492.5**	**493.4**	**1 008.7**

Source: UNDP, *Human Development Indicators 2001*; The World Bank, *World Development Indicators 2002*.

Figure 9.3. Annual fiscal cost of eliminating child labour compared
to other annual costs, in $billion PPP

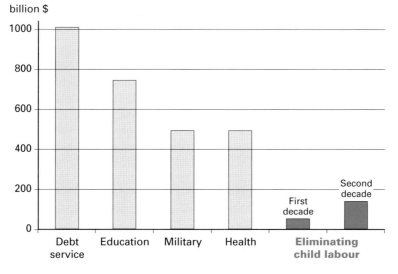

decade could be financed by an average 7.4% increase in the aggregate public
education budget in regions 2-6; the corresponding amount for the second
decade is 18.2%. If child labour elimination were added to social expenditures in general, encompassing both health and education, the increase would
be 4.4% and 11% respectively. These are not impossible increases over current spending, particularly when potential economic growth is taken into account, but they would be difficult to finance all the same. Of course, averages
such as these conceal large differences in the financial capacities of different
countries. While middle-income countries are better placed to assume this

89

additional burden, low-income countries are not. In fact, if this latter group were to increase taxes to meet these obligations, they might exacerbate child labour if the effect of decreasing the disposable income of taxpaying households outweighed the effect on programme beneficiaries (Rogers and Swinnerton, 2001).

Aside from simply increasing public sector resources, three alternative sources of funding suggest themselves.

1) Budgetary transfers. Countries could transfer funds from other budget items to social expenditures. One benchmark that indicates the potential scope for such actions is column 4 of Table 9-4, military spending. If coordinated reductions could be achieved across all countries, a portion of these funds could be released with little cost (or even positive gain) to security. The average fiscal burden in the first decade represents 11.1% of year 2000 military spending in these five regions; the average in the second decade represents 27.5%.

2) Debt relief. Virtually all of the countries considered in this study are net external debtors. Column 5 of Table 9.4 reports their payments, largely to creditors in Region 1. The negative effects of these flows on macroeconomic prospects in the developing world, as well as on the stability of global finance, are well known, and there have been continuing discussions on the potential scope and mechanisms of debt writedowns. One concern of creditors has been to link reductions in debt to increased domestic spending on items that will further the provision of basic needs to the poorest members of the world community, as well as promote economic growth. The model described in this study addresses both of these concerns, and would provide an alternative that debtors and creditors alike might find attractive. The average public sector cost during the first decade represents 5.4% of the aggregate debt service flow reported in 2000; the average for the second decade represents 13.5%.

3) Development assistance. Funds already transferred from rich to poor countries could be augmented and consolidated to meet financing gaps during the first decade of the programme. According the UNDP (2002), net official development assistance in 2000 amounted to $54.9 billion. While sufficient to provide a significant portion of the net financial costs of child labour elimination during the first few years, it currently falls well short of what would be required to meet the needs during the period of greatest impact. Similarly, the global financial assistance targeted at prevention, care and orphan support in connection with HIV/AIDS, proposed by UNAIDS (2002), reaches a peak of approximately $14.5 billion in 2007, well below the funding needs identified by this study.

While each of the above funding vehicles was considered separately, a realistic approach to financing the elimination of child labour would take most or all of them into account. When their combined potential is compared to the cost, it is clear that the feasibility of implementing a model such as ours is not in doubt. Indeed, when reflecting on the elements of the model – universal education through lower secondary school, an urgent elimination of the worst forms of child labour (including rehabilitation when necessary), and an income transfer programme in every country that would replace most of the lost value of child labour –, this conclusion may be both surprising and reassuring.

DATA LIMITATIONS AND AREAS FOR FUTURE RESEARCH

As we have made clear in prior chapters we were faced with several data limitations in key areas of our study. Here we are recapitulating the most important ones, emphasizing the urgent need for further research to fill these gaps.

- ○ **Value of child labour:** While data on adult wages are widely available, data on the wages earned by children of different ages in different occupations are virtually non-existent. Such information is essential for calculating the benefits of child labour to the household and estimating the necessary income transfers to compensate parents for the opportunity costs of their children's schooling. For our study, the few observations from our country studies were insufficient for extrapolation, and we had to resort to estimating child wages as a fraction of unskilled adults' wages. However, this must be regarded as merely a guess of children's actual wages. We require more data on the wage and productivity of children, broken down by age and gender.

- ○ **Ongoing surveys:** Household surveys are typically a one-off affair, providing a snapshot of child labour without permitting the investigation of changing trends in child labour (the annual national household survey PNAD in Brazil being a notable exception). Thus, it is difficult to assess how economic factors alter child labour. This hampered our study's ability to determine the prescribed size of income transfers, and it also required us to merge together observations from different time periods. There is an evident need for time-series data on child labour.

- ○ **Education quality:** The indicators proposed in this study, pupil-teacher ratios and non-personnel expenditures, are input measures and must be considered as rough approximations at best of the quality of education in countries around the world. Their relevance for programmes designed to prevent children from working is far from clear (Matz, 2003). Instead, what is urgently needed are outcome measures derived from standardized tests, which are related to children's school attendance. These could include literacy and numeracy, as well as other school-imparted skills and competences. The OECD's Programme on

International Student Assessment (PISA) may be in important milestone in this endeavour.

○ **Lower secondary education:** A lot of attention has been given to primary education in previous decades, which is indeed very important, as we have discussed. However, from the point of view of IPEC, children up to the age of 14 must be provided with a viable alternative to child labour, and therefore primary education alone is not sufficient. Unfortunately, little is known about school attendance rates at this level (Matz, 2003); where data is reported, it often pertains to secondary education as a whole, which skews the results. More information is also needed on the factors that determine a household's decision whether or not to allow a child's transition from primary to secondary school. The latter issue may be related to potential increases in the value of child labour as the child grows older and is thus connected to another research bottleneck.

○ **Health outcomes:** Very little is known about the impact of child labour in various occupations on children's health, particularly in developing countries. This is true for the effects of hazardous work on children's present health status, but also (and even more so) for the future health consequences of these activities. Longitudinal studies are called for to alleviate this research gap. Similarly, the future health benefits flowing from improved education are not yet documented well enough. This lack of information presented a serious obstacle for our estimation of the benefits of eliminating child labour. Besides their potential contribution to future studies like this one, more complete health data can play a role in helping direct resources to those children in the most pressing need of intervention.

When attempting a large-scale accounting project such as the current study, the lack of critical data can appear as an obstacle to success. On the other hand, one of the main purposes of our work was, by making strenuous demands on the existing information base, to expose its gaps and weaknesses.

Ashenfelter, Orley and Cecilia Rouse. 2000. "Schooling, Intelligence and Income in America". In Kenneth Arrow, Samuel Bowles and Steven Durlauf (eds), *Meritocracy and Economic Inequality*. Princeton: Princeton University Press.

Basu, Kausik and P. H. Van. 1998. "The Economics of Child Labor". *American Economic Review,* p. 412-427.

Beegle, Kathleen, Rajeev H. Dehejia and Roberta Gatti. 2003. *Child Labor, Income Shocks and Access to Credit.* World Bank Policy Research Working Paper 3075.

Bennell, Paul. 1996. "Using and Abusing Rates of Return: A Critique of the World Bank's 1995 Education Sector Review". *International Journal of Educational Development.* 16(3): 235-48.

Bonnel, R. 2000. "HIV/AIDS and Economic Growth: A Global Perspective". *South African Journal of Economics*, 65(5): 820-55.

Brossard, Mathieu and Luc-Charles Gacougnolle. Forthcoming. *Financing Primary Education for All: Yesterday, Today and Tomorrow.* Paris: UNESCO.

Bruns, Barbara, Alain Mingat and Ramahatra Rakotomalala. 2003. *Achieving Universal Primary Education by 2015: A Chance for Every Child.* Washington: The World Bank.

Colclough, Cristopher, and Keith Lewin. 1993. *Educating All the Children: Strategies for Primary Schooling in the South.* Oxford: Clarendon Press.

Dehejia, Rajeev H. and Roberta Gatti. 2002. *Child Labor: The Role of Income Variability and Credit Constraints Across Countries.* National Bureau of Economic Research Working Paper No. 9018.

Delamonica, Enrique, Santosh Mehrotra, and Jan Vandemoortele. 2001. *Is Education for All Affordable? Estimating its Global Minimum Cost.* UNICEF Staff Working Paper No. EPP-01-001. New York: UNICEF.

Dorman, Peter. 2000. *The Economics of Health, Safety, and Well-Being at Work: An Overview.* Geneva: ILO. http://www.ilo.org/public/english/protection/safework/papers/ecoanal/ecoview.htm.

Dorman, Peter. 2001. *Child Labour in the Developed Economies.* Geneva: ILO. http://www.ilo.org/public/english/standards/ipec/publ/policy/index.htm.

Fassa, Anaclaudia. 2003. *Health Benefits of Eliminating Child Labour.* Geneva: ILO.

Freeman, Richard B. and Remco H. Oostendorp. 2000. *Wages Around the World: Pay Across Occupations and Countries.* Cambridge MA: National Bureau of Economic Research.

Gallup, John L. and Jeffrey D. Sachs, 2000. "The Economic Burden of Malaria." CID Working Paper 52. Cambridge, MA: Center for International Development, Harvard University.

Habermalz, Steffen. 2003. "An Examination of Sheepskin Effects Over Time". Institute for the Study of Labor (IZA) Discussion Paper No. 725.

Heywood, John S. 1994. "How Widespread are Sheepskin Returns to Education in the U.S.?" *Economics of Education Review.* 13(3): 227–34.

Hungerford, Thomas and Gary Solon. 1987. "Sheepskin Effects in the Returns to Education". *Review of Economics and Statistics.* 69(1): 175–77.

ILO. 2002. *Every Child Counts: New Global Estimates on Child Labour.* Geneva: ILO.

ILO. 1998. *Statistics on Working Children and Hazardous Child Labour in Brief.* Geneva: ILO.

Jaeger, David A. and Marianne E. Page. 1996. "Degrees Matter: New Evidence on Sheepskin Effects in the Returns to Education". *Review of Economics and Statistics.* 77(4): 733-39.

Knight, J.B. 1979. "Job Competition, Occupational Production Functions, and Filtering Down". *Oxford Economic Papers.* 31: 187-204.

Krueger, Alan B. and Mikael Lindahl. 2001. "Education for Growth: Why and For Whom?" *The Journal of Economic Literature.* 39(4).

Leigh, J. Paul, Steven Markowitz, Marianne Fahs, Chonggak Shin, and Philip Landrigan. 1996. *Costs of Occupational Injuries and Illnesses.* NIOHS Report U60/CCU902886.

Levison, Deborah, Jasper Hoek, David Lam and Suzanne Duryea. 2002. *Implications of Intermittent Employment for Child Labor Estimates.* Unpublished manuscript.

Matz, Peter. 2003. *Costs and Benefits of Education to Eliminate Child Labour.* Geneva: ILO.

McCarthy, F. Desmond, Holger Wolf and Yi Wu. 1999. *The Growth Costs of Malaria.* Unpublished manuscript.

Mehrotra, Santosh, and Jan Vandemoortele. 1997. *Cost and Financing of Primary Education: Options for Reform in Sub-Saharan Africa.* UNICEF Staff Working Paper No. EVL-97-006. New York: UNICEF.

Mincer, Jacob. 1974. *Schooling, Experience and Earnings.* New York: National Bureau of Economic Research.

OECD/UNESCO. 2001. *Teachers for Tomorrow's Schools: Analysis of the World Education Indicators.* Paris: OECD/UNESCO-UIS.

Psacharopoulos, George, and Harry A. Patrinos. 2002. *Returns to Investment in Education: A Further Update.* World Bank Policy Research Working Paper 2881. Washington: The World Bank.

Psacharopoulos, George. 1999. *The Opportunity Cost of Child Labour: A Review of the Benefits of Education.* Washington: U.S. Department of Labor, Bureau of International Labor Affairs.

Ranjan, Priya. 2001. "Credit Constraints and the Phenomenon of Child Labor". *Journal of Development Economics.* 64: 81-102.

Rogers, Carol Ann and Kenneth Swinnerton. 2001. *Inequality, Productivity and Child Labor: Theory and Evidence.* Unpublished manuscript.

Schady, Norbert. R. 2000. *Convexity and Sheepskin Effects in the Human Capital Earnings Function: Recent Evidence for Filipino Men.* Washington: World Bank Education Working Paper No. 2566.

Shabbir, Tayyeb. 1991. "Sheepskin Effects in the Returns to Education in a Developing Country". *The Pakistan Development Review.* 30(1): 1-19.

Spence, Michael. 1973. "Job Market Signaling". *Quarterly Journal of Economics.* 87(3): 355-79.

Suwal, Bhim Raj, Bal Kumar KC and Keshab Prasad Adhikari. 1997. *Child Labour Situation in Nepal.* Kathmandu: ILO.

Thurow, Lester. 1975. *Generating Inequality: Mechanisms of Distribution in the U.S. Economy.* New York: Basic Books.

Ueda, Misaki A. 2002. *The Unit Costs of Programmes to Prevent or End Child Labour: A Review of Selected ILO/IPEC Programme Interventions.* Geneva: ILO.

UN 2000. *World Population Prospects, 2000 Revision.* New York: UN Population Division, Department of Social and Economic Affairs.

UNAIDS. 2002. *Financial Resources for HIV/AIDS Programmes in Low- and Middle-Income Countries over the Next Five Years.* UNAIDS/PCB (13)/02.5

UNDP. 2002. *Human Development Indicators 2002.* New York: UNDP.

UNDP. 2001. *Human Development Indicators 2001.* New York: UNDP.

UNDP. 2000. *Mozambique National Human Development Report.* New York: UNDP.

UNICEF. 2003. *The State of the World's Children 2003.* New York: UNICEF.

WHO. 2003. *Global Burden of Disease 2000.* http://www3.who.int/whosis/menu.cfm?path=evidence,burden,burden_estimates,burden_estimates_2000V2&language=english

WHO. 2002. *Summary Measures of Population Health: Concepts, Ethics, Measurement and Applications.* http://www.who.int/pub/smph/en/index.html.

Wolff, Laurence, Ernesto Schiefelbein and Jorge Valenzuela. 1994. *Improving the Quality of Primary Education in Latin America and the Caribbean: Toward the 21st century.* World Bank Discussion Paper, Education and Training Series. Washington DC: The World Bank.

The World Bank. 2002. *Education and HIV/AIDS: A Window of Hope.* Washington: The World Bank.

The World Bank. 2002a. *World Development Indicators 2002.* Washington: The World Bank.a

COUNTRIES EMPLOYED
FOR REGIONAL EXTRAPOLATION

The following 36 countries were eliminated from the study, either because they were deemed high income, or because data were generally unavailable for them: Australia, Austria, Belgium, Canada, Cape Verde, Channel Islands, Denmark, East Timor, Finland, France, Germany, Greece, Guadeloupe, Iceland, Ireland, Italy, Japan, Luxembourg, Macao SAR, Malta, Martinique, Netherlands, Netherlands Antilles, New Zealand, Norway, Occ. Palestinian Territories, Portugal, Reunion, Saint Lucia, Slovenia, Spain, Sweden, Switzerland, United Kingdom, USA, Western Sahara.

This left two countries in Region 1, Cyprus and Turkey. We incorporated them in Region 6 (Middle East and North Africa).

The final composition of regions was as follows:

Region 2: Albania, Armenia, Azerbaijan, Belarus, Bosnia and Herzegovina, Bulgaria, Croatia, Czech Republic, Estonia, Georgia, Hungary, Kazakhstan, Kyrgyzstan, Latvia, Lithuania, Macedonia, Moldova, Poland, Romania, Russian Federation, Slovakia, Tajikistan, Turkmenistan, Ukraine, Uzbekistan, Yugoslavia

Region 3: Afghanistan, Bangladesh, Bhutan, Brunei Darussalam, Cambodia, China, Fiji, French Polynesia, Guam, Hong Kong SAR, India, Indonesia, Laos, Malaysia, Maldives, Mongolia, Myanmar, Nepal, New Caledonia, North Korea, Pakistan, Papua New Guinea, Philippines, Samoa, Singapore, Solomon Islands, South Korea, Sri Lanka, Thailand, Vanuatu, Viet Nam

Region 4: Argentina, Bahamas, Barbados, Belize, Bolivia, Brazil, Chile, Colombia, Costa Rica, Cuba, Dominican Republic, Ecuador, El Salvador, French Guiana, Guatemala, Guyana, Haiti, Honduras, Jamaica, Mexico, Nicaragua, Panama, Paraguay, Peru, Puerto Rico, Suriname, Trinidad and Tobago, Uruguay, Venezuela

Region 5: Angola, Benin, Botswana, Burkina Faso, Burundi, Cameroon, Central African Republic, Chad, Comoros, Congo, Côte d'Ivoire, Dem. Rep.

of the Congo, Equatorial Guinea, Eritrea, Ethiopia, Gabon, Gambia, Ghana, Guinea, Guinea-Bissau, Kenya, Lesotho, Liberia, Madagascar, Malawi, Mali, Mauritania, Mauritius, Mozambique, Namibia, Niger, Nigeria, Rwanda, Senegal, Sierra Leone, Somalia, South Africa, Swaziland, Tanzania, Togo, Uganda, Zambia, Zimbabwe

Region 6: Algeria, Bahrain, Cyprus, Djibouti, Egypt, Iran, Iraq, Israel, Jordan, Kuwait, Lebanon, Libya, Morocco, Oman, Qatar, Saudi Arabia, Sudan, Syria, Tunisia, Turkey, United Arab Emirates, Yemen

Two sets of variables were employed in this study, core and auxiliary. The core variables were those directly utilized in cost and benefit calculations. Auxiliary variables were of use solely for the purpose of enabling the imputation of missing core observations. All economic variables were converted to $PPP for year 2000 using World Bank conversion factors.

Tables A2.1 and A2.2 indicate the sources for these variables.

Countries fell into three general categories: those studied by our country teams, for which data were virtually complete; those with household surveys, primarily based on the methodology of IPEC (SIMPOC) or the World Bank (LSMS), for which we had observations on most but not all variables; and the remainder, who were represented to varying extents in publicly reported data sets. The middle category, which overlaps partially with the first, consisted of the following countries:

○ Transitional countries: Azerbaijan, Kazakhstan, Ukraine

○ Asia: Bangladesh, Cambodia, India, Pakistan, Philippines, Sri Lanka

○ Latin America and the Caribbean: Bolivia, Brazil, Colombia, Costa Rica, El Salvador, Mexico, Paraguay

○ Sub-Saharan Africa: Cameroon, Ghana, Kenya, Mauritania, Namibia, Nigeria, Senegal, South Africa, Zambia

○ Middle East and North Africa: Egypt, Turkey (added from Europe), Yemen

The imputation proceeded sequentially. Variables with few missing observations were completed first; then they were used to assist in the imputation of other variables. The preferred method was multivariate regression. Regressions were selected on the basis of explanatory power (adjusted R^2) and the plausibility and significance of individual coefficients. Neighbourhood imputation and regional averaging were employed as necessary. In a few instances, outliers were trimmed. The rest of this section describes the methods in greater detail.

Table A2.1. Core variables

Variable	Source
Working children 5-11	SIMPOC
Working children 12-14	SIMPOC
Value of child labour	SIMPOC, C/B Country studies
Families with school age children in poverty	SIMPOC, LSMS
Poverty gap	LSMS, C/B Country studies
School age children per family	SIMPOC, LSMS, C/B Country studies
Net attendance rate in primary education	SIMPOC, UNICEF
Net attendance rate in secondary education	SIMPOC, UNICEF
Unit recurrent cost education	C/B Country studies
Unit capital cost of primary education	C/B Country studies
Unit capital cost of secondary education	C/B Country studies
Unit cost of intervention	IPEC
Unconditional worst forms children	IPEC
Socially excluded children	UNHCR, Nepal country study
Children in hazardous work	SIMPOC
Worst forms DALYs	SIMPOC, IPEC
Average unskilled wage	LABORSTA
Population ages 6-11, 2000	World Bank
Population ages 6-11, 2015	World Bank
Population ages 6-11, 2020	World Bank
Population ages 12-14, 2000	World Bank
Population ages 12-14, 2005	World Bank
Population ages 12-14, 2020	World Bank
GNI per capita	WDI

Table A2.2. Auxiliary variables

Variable	Source
Dependency ratio, 5-11	Generated from core variables
Dependency ratio, 12-14	Generated from core variables
Dependency ratio, 5-14	Generated from core variables
Life epectancy at 15, 2000–2005	WDI
Education expenditures, % of GNP	WDI
Health expenditures, % of GDP	WDI
Pupil teacher ratio, primary	WDI
Gini coefficient	CIA World Fact Book, World Bank
Total fertility rate	WDI
Pupil teacher ratio, secondary	WDI
Illiteracy rate	WDI
Mortality rate	WDI

1) Gini (GINI). Neighbourhood methods were used to extend this variable, for which we initially had 94 observations. Data are for various years between 1990-97.

2) GNI per capita. Population data are from the World Bank, as are data on Gross National Income, both for the year 2000. Missing observations (17) were drawn from the CIA World Fact Book series on GNP. There is potential for error in the range of 25% above or below GNI in this procedure.

3) Populations 6-11, 12-14. These were adapted from World Bank data using triangular adjustments. This method assumes equal yearly increments over the age ranges being measured. Thus, the average for a reported range is assigned to the midpoint of that range, with annual increments calculated based on the ratio of midpoints.

4) Average unskilled wage. The LABORSTA data have been compiled by Freeman and Oostendorp (2000). From this source, we extracted the following occupations as representative of unskilled labour: field crop farm worker, plantation worker, forestry worker, deep sea fisherman, miner, underground helper, meat packer, thread and yarn, spinner, labourer (industry: spinning), garment cutter, wood grinder, labourer (industry: printing), labourer (industry: manufacturing, except chemicals), labourer (industry: manufacturing, chemical products), labourer (industry: metal and steel), labourer (industry: manufacturing, machinery), labourer (industry: electric, light power), bricklayer, construction, labourer (industry: construction). There were 77 observations in all, with countries reporting various years during the period 1990-99, and not all occupations reported for each country. We represented each country's unskilled wage as the unweighted average of the detailed occupations for which data were available. (By "unskilled" in this context is meant work available to individuals with limited formal

Table A2.3. Imputation regression for dependent variable, average unskilled wage (t-statistic in parentheses)

Variable	Coefficient
Constant	3441.68
	(2.95)
GNI-PC	0.317
	(6.20)
GNP-ED	18 773.46
	(1.53)
GNP-HEALTH	133.02
	(1.54)
GINI	-80.05
	(-3.91)
Adj. R^2	0.87
N=24	

schooling.) Many of the observations constructed in this manner appeared unreliable in light of economic data from WDI. We dropped all data points with significant discrepancies, after which 25 remained. These were used as the basis for a regression to impute the rest.

Table A2.3 reports the regression on this variable.

All signs are appropriate: the average unskilled wage is increasing in per capita income and the percentages of income spent on education and health; it is decreasing in inequality (GINI) and fertility (school age children per household).

5) Working children 5-14. As described more fully in Chapter 3, we utilized 28 observations from the data on which *Every Child Counts* (ILO, 2002) was based, also employing the same set of adjustments. We extrapolated to the remaining countries on the basis of the unweighted regional averages of working children to the total of all children between these ages.

6) Families with school age children in poverty. We initially had 11 observations on this variable. To avoid spurious results, it was converted into a ratio whose denominator was the combined populations of children ages 6 to 11 and 12 to 14 in 2000. Table A2.4 reports the regression model employed.

Table A2.4. Imputation regression on dependent variable, ratio of families with school age children in poverty to population ages 6 to 14 (t-statistic in parentheses)

Variable	Coefficient
Constant	-0.01 (-0.01)
GNI-PC	-0.0004 (-2.84)
GINI	0.008 (3.07)
Region2	0.15 (1.92)
Adj. R^2	0.42
N=11	

Signs are appropriate: higher per capita income results in fewer poor families; greater inequality results in more. A dummy variable for transitional countries proved significant, reflecting the income pressure on households during the 1990s. The estimated ratio was multiplied by the corresponding age population to yield the final result.

7) Poverty gap. We had 21 observations, which we denominated by GNI per capita for regression purposes. Table A2.5 reports this model.

Table A2.5. Imputation regression on dependent variable,
ratio of poverty gap to GNI per capita (t-statistic in parentheses)

Variable	Coefficient
Constant	-0.236 (-1.56)
TFR	0.025 (1.95)
GNP-ED	-0.886 (-1.49)
LE-15	0.005 (2.08)
Region5	0.151 (2.70)
Adj. R^2	0.68
N=21	

Most variables are appropriately signed. Higher fertility is associated with deeper poverty; expenditures on education are associated with smaller poverty gaps. Africa has deeper poverty even controlling for other factors. Only the coefficient on life expectancy is counterintuitive, perhaps capturing influences on the setting of national poverty lines. The estimated value of this ratio was multiplied by GNI per capita to yield an estimate of absolute poverty gap.

8) School-age children per family. Table A2.6 reports the regression model used to impute this series.

Table A2.6. Imputation regression on dependent variable,
school age children per family (t-statistic in parentheses)

Variable	Coefficient
Constant	2.963 (6.99)
ILLITRATE	0.013 (2.13)
GNI-PC	-0.001 (-3.18)
GNI-PCSQ E-08	4.39 (2.74)
Adj. R^2	0.67
N=13	

A higher illiteracy rate is associated with larger family size; the opposite relationship holds for GNI per capita, with curvature picked up by the squared term.

9) Unit cost of intervention. Table A2.7 reports the regression model used to impute this series.

Table A2.7. Imputation regression on dependent variable,
unit cost of intervention (t-statistic in parentheses)

Variable	Coefficient
Constant	-1004.431
	(-0.58)
GNI-PC	-0.218
	(-3.02)
GINI	-57.471
	(-2.84)
DEPRAT12-14	44 296.44
	(2.21)
Region 4	2137.163
	(5.08)
Adj. R^2	0.85
N=16	

Higher per capita income is associated with lower intervention costs, as is greater income inequality. Higher ratios of children ages 12 to 14 to total population are associated with higher intervention costs. Latin America tends to have higher costs, since a larger percentage of programmes in that region targeted children in prostitution, a problem for which solutions are relatively more resource-intensive.

10) Net enrolment rates, primary and lower secondary education. Procedures for extrapolating the initial set of observations are described in Chapter 4.

11) Unit recurrent cost of education. We had eight observations on this variable, all generated by our country teams. Two appeared to be outliers; the

Table A2.8. Imputation regression on dependent variable,
ratio of unit recurrent costs of education to GNI per capita
(t-statistic in parentheses)

Variable	Coefficient
Constant	0.512
	(1.95)
ln GNI-PC	-0.051
	(-1.51)
Adj. R^2	0.20
N=6	

other six were modestly correlated with ln GNI per capita. Table A2.8 reports a simple regression of the ratio of unit recurrent costs to ln GNI per capita on ln GNI per capita itself.

The sign on the natural log of per capita income is what one would expect: personnel and related costs of supplying education do not vary to the extent that per capita income does, thus poorer countries have a higher ratio of unit recurrent costs to GNI per capita than wealthier countries do. The natural log of income was selected because it produces more plausible results for higher-income countries, particularly those whose income per capita exceeds all six of our observations. Nevertheless, the formula did not perform adequately for the 33 countries with income per capita above $8,500; in theses cases the ratio of unit recurrent costs to ln GNI per capita was truncated at 5%.

12) Unit capital costs of education. We had eight observations on this variable, four of which included different values for primary and secondary levels. Since there were too few observations incorporating this distinction, and since there appeared to be no relationship governing the ratio of primary to secondary costs in these four cases, we converted them into average unit costs, weighted by the corresponding age populations. Moreover, there was no systematic variation in the full set of observations that could be used as a basis for extrapolation. We found a substantial range, from 0.7 to 4.8, in the ratios of unit capital to unit recurrent costs and chose to use this as the basis for low, medium and high estimates. First, the same two outliers were deleted. The low estimate was established near the bottom end of the remaining range; this proved to be approximately 1. (That is, for these observations, the ratio of unit capital to unit recurrent costs was unity.) The high estimate was 4.8. For the medium estimate, we took a simple average of the ratios for these six observations; it came to approximately 2.25. These ratios were applied to the estimates for recurrent costs in the remaining countries to generate estimates for unit capital costs.

13) Worst form DALYs. From the 20 observations, computed in the manner described in Chapter 8, we eliminated three due to a lack of other data needed for regression. We also transformed the dependent variable (DALYs) by denominating it by the population of children ages 6 to 14. The model selected and its results are presented in Table A2.9.

The coefficients are presented three decimal places to the right because the ratio of DALYs to child population is very low. (The mean of the dependent variable is 0.003.) We also considered regional dummies, two of which proved to be significant. Unfortunately, there are no unambiguous theoretical relationships between these variables and our estimates of the DALY ratio. The industrial composition of child labour in the transitional countries yields higher predicted DALYs and that of North Africa and the Middle East lower. Illiteracy and the percent of social expenditures are

Table A2.9. Imputation regression for dependent variable, ratio of worst form DALYs to the population of children ages 6 to 14 (t-statistic in parentheses)

Variable	Coefficient ($\times$ 1000)
Constant	-0.485
	(-0.48)
ILLITRATE	0.115
	(8.28)
AVEWAGE	-0.002
	(-6.70)
GDP-HEALTH	0.406
	(3.99)
GNP-EDUCATION	88.071
	(5.18)
REGION6	-1.926
	(-3.46)
REGION2	3.996
	(3.68)
Adj. R^2	0.85
N=17	

correlated with more DALYs, and average wages with less. These are neither expected nor unexpected. The fit is surprisingly strong overall. The ratios estimated in the above regression were multiplied by the number of children ages 6 to 14 to generate the required DALY estimates.

FORMULAS FOR CALCULATING
COSTS AND BENEFITS

For the purposes of this Annex, the variables entering into the cost and benefit calculations have been abbreviated, as in Table A3.1.

Table A3.1. Abbreviations for core variables

Variable	Abbreviation
Working children 6-11	WC611
Working children 12-14	WC1214
Value of child labour	VCL
Families with school age children in poverty	FSACP
Poverty gap	PG
School age children per family	SACPF
Net attendance rate in primary education	NARP
Net attendance cost in secondary education	NARS
Unit recurrent cost education	URC
Unit capital cost of primary education	UCCP
Unit capital cost of secondary education	UCCS
Unit cost of intervention	UCI
Unconditional worst forms children	UWFC
Socially excluded children	SEC
Children in hazardous work	HWC
Worst forms DALYs	DALYS
Average unskilled wage	AW
Population ages 6-11, 2000	POP611_00
Population ages 6-11, 2015	POP611_15
Population ages 6-11, 2020	POP611_20
Population ages 12-14, 2000	POP1214_00
Population ages 12-14, 2005	POP1214_05
Population ages 12-14, 2020	POP1214_20
GNI per capita	GNIPC
Discount rate	r
Mincerian coefficient	MC
Monetary cost per DALY	MDALY

Calculations take the form either of present values of the entire cost or benefit stream or of undiscounted year-to-year amounts (as reported in Chapter 9). Here we will present the methodology for the present values first and then the undiscounted yearly values.

A. DISCOUNTED PRESENT VALUES

1. Opportunity cost of child labour.

The undiscounted growth rate of this variable is

$$g = \sqrt[20]{\frac{(POP611\_20 + POP1214\_20)*20}{(POP611\_00 + POP1214\_00)}}$$

since there are two sources of growth, the population growth of the relevant age group and the increase in child labour prevented from 1/20 of its amount in the first year to the total amount in the twentieth.

Let $a = \dfrac{g}{1+r}$

Then the opportunity cost is given by:

$$\left[\frac{(WC611 + WC1214)*VCL}{20}\right]*\frac{(1-a^5)}{1-a} \quad \text{in Wave 1.}$$

Subsequent waves are:

$$\text{Wave 2:} \quad OC = \left[\frac{(WC611 + WC1214)*VCL}{20}\right]*\frac{(1-a^5)}{1-a}*a^5$$

$$\text{Wave 3:} \quad OC = \left[\frac{(WC611 + WC1214)*VCL}{20}\right]*\frac{(1-a^{10})}{1-a}*a^{15}$$

$$\text{Wave 4:} \quad OC = \left[\frac{(WC611 + WC1214)*VCL}{20}\right]*\frac{(1-a^{10})}{1-a}*a^{15}$$

2. Cost of the income transfer programme

The main cost of the income transfer programme is the transfer itself. To compute this, we first calculate the total transfer indicated by the formula discussed in Chapter 5.

If $.8 * VCL * SACPF \leq PG$ then transfer $= .8 * VCL * SACPF * FSACP$

If $.6 * VCL * SACPF < PG$ then transfer $= PG * FSACP$

Otherwise transfer $= .6 * VCL * SACPF * FSACP$

We did not factor in a growth rate based on population, given the uncertainty surrounding family size and poverty rates; hence the growth factor $g = 1.1616$ (the twentieth root of 20). As before,

$$a = \frac{g}{1+r}$$

Therefore the wave calculations for the income transfer are:

Wave 1: $\left(\dfrac{\text{transfer}}{20}\right) * \left(\dfrac{1-a^5}{1-a}\right)$

Wave 2: $\left(\dfrac{\text{transfer}}{20}\right) * \left(\dfrac{1-a^5}{1-a}\right) * a^5$

Wave 3: $\left(\dfrac{\text{transfer}}{20}\right) * \left(\dfrac{1-a^5}{1-a}\right) * a^{10}$

Wave 4: $\left(\dfrac{\text{transfer}}{20}\right) * \left(\dfrac{1-a^5}{1-a}\right) * a^{15}$

The administrative (real resource) cost is calculated at 5% of the transfer amount.

3. Programme intervention cost

This item is discussed in Chapter 6. There is no growth rate anticipated for the number of children to be targeted by these interventions; exact head-counts are used, even though they are not representative. Hence:

$$a = \frac{1}{1+r}$$

and the wave calculations are

Wave 1: $0.1*(SEC + UWFC + HWC)*UCI*\left(\frac{1-a^5}{1-a}\right)$

Wave 2: $0.1*(SEC + UWFC + HWC)*UCI*\left(\frac{1-a^5}{1-a}\right)*a^5$

4. Cost of primary education

Capital and recurrent costs are handled differently, since only the latter is cumulative. We begin with recurrent costs.

The growth rate for the first three waves is

$$g = \sqrt[15]{\frac{POP611\_15*20}{POP611\_00}}$$

and once more

$$a = \frac{g}{1+r}$$

Thus the corresponding wave formulas are

Wave 1: $\left(\frac{UCR*(1-NARP)*POP611\_00}{15}\right)*\left(\frac{1-a^5}{1-a}\right)$

Wave 2: $\left(\frac{UCR*(1-NARP)*POP611\_00}{15}\right)*\left(\frac{1-a^5}{1-a}\right)*a^5$

Wave 3: $\left(\frac{UCR*(1-NARP)*POP611\_00}{15}\right)*\left(\frac{1-a^5}{1-a}\right)*a^{10}$

Wave 4 must be calculated somewhat differently, since there is no growth occurring due to an increase in the percentage of the age group being served. For this wave,

$$g = \sqrt[5]{\frac{POP611\_20}{POP611\_15}}$$

and there is no change in the formula for a. Utilizing the new value for a,

Wave 4: $UCR * (1 - NERP) * POP611\_15 * \left(\frac{1 - a^5}{1 - a}\right) * a^{15}$

There are only three waves for capital costs. The only source of growth derives from population:

$$g = \sqrt[15]{\frac{POP611\_15}{POP611\_00}}$$

Thus the waves are calculated as

Wave 1: $\left(\frac{UCCP * (1 - NARP) * POP611\_00}{15}\right) * \left(\frac{1 - a^5}{1 - a}\right)$

Wave 2: $\left(\frac{UCCP * (1 - NARP) * POP611\_00}{15}\right) * \left(\frac{1 - a^5}{1 - a}\right) * a^5$

Wave 3: $\left(\frac{UCCP * (1 - NARP) * POP611\_00}{15}\right) * \left(\frac{1 - a^5}{1 - a}\right) * a^{10}$

5. Costs of secondary education

There are only three waves, with the first beginning in 2005.
For recurrent costs,

$$g = \sqrt[15]{\frac{POP1214\_20 * 15}{POP1214\_05}}$$

Since growth in the variable commences in wave 2, we can distinguish between two values of a:

$$a_1 = \frac{g}{1+r} \qquad a_2 = \frac{1}{1+r}$$

Then the wave calculations become

Wave 2:
$$\left(\frac{UCR * (1-NARS) * POP1214\_05}{15}\right) * a_2^5 * \left(\frac{1-a_1^5}{1-a_1}\right)$$

Wave 3:
$$\left(\frac{UCR * (1-NARS) * POP1214\_05}{15}\right) * a_2^5 * a_1^5 * \left(\frac{1-a_1^5}{1-a_1}\right)$$

Wave 4:
$$\left(\frac{UCR * (1-NARS) * POP1214\_05}{15}\right) * a_2^5 * a_1^{10} * \left(\frac{1-a_1^5}{1-a_1}\right)$$

For capital costs,

$$g = \sqrt[15]{\frac{POP1214\_20}{POP1214\_05}}$$

and a_1 and a_2 are calculated as above.

The wave calculations are:

Wave 2:
$$\left(\frac{UCCS * (1-NARS) * POP1214\_05}{15}\right) * a_2^5 * \left(\frac{1-a_1^5}{1-a_1}\right)$$

Wave 3:
$$\left(\frac{UCCS * (1-NARS) * POP1214\_05}{15}\right) * a_2^5 * a_1^5 * \left(\frac{1-a_1^5}{1-a_1}\right)$$

Wave 4:
$$\left(\frac{UCCS * (1-NARS) * POP1214\_05}{15}\right) * a_2^5 * a_1^{10} * \left(\frac{1-a_1^5}{1-a_1}\right)$$

6. Benefits of education

Consider first primary education. The growth rate in the number of student-years to be valued is

$$g = \sqrt[15]{\frac{POP611\_15 * 15}{POP611\_00}}$$

because they are cumulative. This yields values for a_1 and a_2 as before. For the wave calculations, we assume that benefits begin 6 years after the average student-year is acquired and accrue over a 40-year period. (We do not adjust for the fraction of students expected to complete additional years of education following primary school.) Hence:

Wave 1: $\left(\dfrac{MC * AW * (1 - NARP) * POP611\_00}{15}\right) * \left(\dfrac{1 - a_1^{5}}{1 - a_1}\right) * a_2^{6} * \left(\dfrac{1 - a_2^{40}}{1 - a_2}\right)$

Wave 2: $\left(\dfrac{MC * AW * (1 - NARP) * POP611\_00}{15}\right) * a_1^{5} * \left(\dfrac{1 - a_1^{5}}{1 - a_1}\right) * a_2^{6} * \left(\dfrac{1 - a_2^{40}}{1 - a_2}\right)$

Wave 3: $\left(\dfrac{MC * AW * (1 - NARP) * POP611\_00}{15}\right) * a_1^{10} * \left(\dfrac{1 - a_1^{5}}{1 - a_1}\right) * a_2^{6} * \left(\dfrac{1 - a_2^{40}}{1 - a_2}\right)$

Wave 4: $MC * AW * (1 - NARP) * POP611\_15 * a_2^{21} * \left(\dfrac{1 - a_2^{5}}{1 - a_2}\right) * \left(\dfrac{1 - a_2^{40}}{1 - a_2}\right)$

(Population growth between 2015 and 2020 is not incorporated to simplify the expression.)

Secondary education is calculated equivalently, with the exception that work is assumed to begin two years after the average student-year, and there is no first wave. Thus

$$g = \sqrt[15]{\frac{POP1214\_20 * 15}{POP1214\_05}}$$

with corresponding a_1 and a_2.

This yields the wave formulas

Wave 2: $\left(\dfrac{MC*AW*(1-NARS)*POP1214\_05}{15}\right)*a_2^{\ 7}*\left(\dfrac{1-a_1^{\ 5}}{1-a_1}\right)*\left(\dfrac{1-a_2^{\ 40}}{1-a_2}\right)$

Wave 3: $\left(\dfrac{MC*AW*(1-NARS)*POP1214\_05}{15}\right)*a_2^{\ 7}*a_1^{\ 5}*\left(\dfrac{1-a_1^{\ 5}}{1-a_1}\right)*\left(\dfrac{1-a_2^{\ 40}}{1-a_2}\right)$

Wave 4: $\left(\dfrac{MC*AW*(1-NARS)*POP1214\_05}{15}\right)*a_2^{\ 7}*a_1^{\ 10}*\left(\dfrac{1-a_1^{\ 5}}{1-a_1}\right)*\left(\dfrac{1-a_2^{\ 40}}{1-a_2}\right)$

7. Health benefits

The growth rate for this variable derives entirely from the cumulative growth over ten years in the benefits accrued; no population growth factor enters in. Hence g = 1.2589, the tenth root of 10, and a_1 and a_2 are as before.

Wave 1: $\left(\dfrac{DALYS*MDALY}{10}\right)*\left(\dfrac{1-a_1^{\ 5}}{1-a_1}\right)$

Wave 2: $\left(\dfrac{DALYS*MDALY}{10}\right)*a_1^{\ 5}*\left(\dfrac{1-a_1^{\ 5}}{1-a_1}\right)$

Wave 3: $DALYS*MDALY*a_2^{\ 10}*\left(\dfrac{1-a_2^{\ 5}}{1-a_2}\right)$

Wave 4: $DALYS*MDALY*a_2^{\ 15}*\left(\dfrac{1-a_2^{\ 5}}{1-a_2}\right)$

B. ANNUAL UNDISCOUNTED FLOWS

The general strategy in this set of calculations is to determine an initial annual increment to cost or benefit and its undiscounted rate of change from year to year. For some variables it is necessary to partition the years due to changes in growth rates. (These series are spline functions.)

1. Opportunity cost

The annual increment is $\dfrac{(WC611 + WC1214) * VCL}{20}$

and $g = \sqrt[20]{\dfrac{POP611\_20 + POP1214\_20}{POP611\_00 + POP1214\_00}}$

Thus year i is calculated as $\left(\text{increment} * g^{i\text{-}1}\right)$.

2. Income transfers

We assume the flow to increase so as to reach an additional 1/20 of the target population in each year. Hence the annual increment is 1/20 of the total transfer calculated as in A2 (the numerator only), and year i is i/20 of this amount.

3. Programme intervention costs

This variable is non-cumulative; therefore the annual flow for the first ten years is 1/10 of the total cost given by multiplying the target population by the unit cost of intervention. There is no cost during the second ten years of the model.

4. Primary education costs

First the recurrent costs. The annual increment is given by

$$\frac{(1-\text{NARP})*\text{POP611}\_00*\text{UCR}}{15}$$

and the growth rate is

$$g = \sqrt[15]{\frac{\text{POP611}\_15*15}{\text{POP611}\_00}}$$

The years 2016-2020 are set equal to 2015; population growth during this period is disregarded for purposes of simpicity.

The capital costs are similar. The annual increment is

$$\frac{(1-\text{NARP})*\text{POP611}\_00*\text{UCCP}}{15}$$

and $\quad g = \sqrt[15]{\dfrac{\text{POP611}\_15}{\text{POP611}\_00}}$

There are no flows during the years 2016-2020.

5. Secondary education costs

These are similar to primary costs, but a different set of years must be calculated. For recurrent costs, the annual increment is

$$\frac{(1-\text{NARS})*\text{POP1214}\_05*\text{UCR}}{15}$$

and $\quad g = \sqrt[15]{\dfrac{\text{POP61214}\_20*15}{\text{POP1214}\_05}}$

For capital costs the corresponding calculations are

$$\frac{(1-\text{NARS})*\text{POP1214}\_05*\text{UCCS}}{15}$$

$$\text{and}\quad g=\sqrt[15]{\frac{\text{POP61214}\_20}{\text{POP1214}\_05}}$$

6. Education benefits

For primary education the annual increment is

$$\frac{(1-\text{NARP})*\text{POP611}\_00*\text{MC}*\text{AW}}{15}$$

$$\text{and}\quad g=\sqrt[15]{\frac{\text{POP611}\_15*15}{\text{POP611}\_00}}$$

Calculation is complicated by the accumulation of benefit years (each student-year engenders a string of benefit years), and the time delay between the acquisition of education and the accrual of benefits. The formula for the benefit in year i is

$$B_i = \text{increment} * g^{i-7} + B_{i-1}$$

for years 7-20 of the model. (Note that, due to the time lag between education and benefits, that the education growth rate for the period 2000-2013 applies to the benefit years 2007-2020.)

Secondary education has nearly the same structure, but with different time parameters. The annual increment is

$$\frac{(1-\text{NARS})*\text{POP1214}\_05*\text{MC}*\text{AW}}{15}$$

$$\text{and}\quad g=\sqrt[15]{\frac{\text{POP1214}\_20*15}{\text{POP1214}\_05}}$$

Similarly,

$$B_i = \text{increment} * g^{i-8} + B_{i-1}$$

since benefits commence in the eighth year of the model.

7. Health benefits

Since DALYs aggregate health outcomes arising over a period of time, additional assumptions must be made to convert the health benefits to annual flows. Taking a conservative position, we assume that 25% of the disability-adjusted outcome occurs during the initial year of injury or illness and that 3% occurs in each subsequent year. (This means that such delayed effects end after 25 years, so that exactly one DALY is accounted for.) Also, we can distinguish between BI_i and B_i, where the first represents an initial DALY exposure in year i and the second the cumulative benefits from year i's initial exposure plus the continuing exposures carried over from previous years.

The annual increment for BI is

$$\frac{DALYS*MDALY}{40}$$

where the denominator incorporates both the ten-year time frame for the elimination of hazardous child labour and the assumption that a fourth of the outcomes are experienced in the initial year. The growth rate is simply 1.2589, then tenth root of ten.

Thus, for the first ten years,

$$BI_i = \text{increment} * g^i$$

$$\text{and} \quad B_i = BI_i + .12 * \sum_{j=1}^{i-1} BI_j$$

where j denotes the years of prior exposure. Note that multiplying by 0.12 takes into account both the 3% annual carryover and the initial division of the DALY by 4 in annual increment formula.

For the second ten years BI_i equals its value in year 10, and the formula for B_i is unchanged.

Annex 4a
COSTS AND BENEFITS
OF ELIMINATING CHILD LABOUR IN BRAZIL

Brazil was one of the eight countries chosen to implement the costs and benefits study of eliminating child labour. The country was selected for its representativeness in the Latin America region, and for the availability of data on child labour. The main source of information used in this study is a National Household Survey (*Pesquisa Nacional por Amostra de Domicílios* – PNAD) undertaken by the Brazilian Geographical and Statistical Institute (IBGE) in 1999. This survey includes more than 330,000 individuals from the Northeast, Southeast, South, Central and the urban part of the North of Brazil. It contains information on the participation of children in the labour force from the age of five, in addition to data on household characteristics, individuals' education, sex, race, age, wages, hours of work, non-earnings income, etc.. The sample design established for the survey allows the expansion of the results to the whole country as well as its regions, states and metropolitan areas.

The use of micro-data allows precise estimates of the required computations. A problem emerges, however, for the rural area of the Northern region, where there are no data collected in PNAD due to access difficulties, except for Tocantins state. In this case, the percentage of working children, poor children, and children in hazardous work in the rural Northeastern region was assumed to be the same as in the rural Northern region, since they are both poor regions. The population in the rural north of Brazil is known from the demographic census 2000.

Another source of information is the school census. Principals from private and public schools at county, state and federal level have provided the following information on an annual basis since 1995: school infrastructure, general information about classroom and personnel, pre-school education, literacy courses, primary school, secondary school, and youths' and adults' education and technical education.

In addition, information on expenditures and government programmes were obtained through the Ministry of Education, Treasury Bureau, and the Ministry of Retirement and Social Assistance.

Despite the legislation prohibiting children below the age of 16 from working in Brazil, data from the 1999 national household survey show that there were four and a half million working children from 5 to 15 years old, which represents more than 12% of the population in this age group. Most of these children live in rural areas and are boys. Many are rural workers, but there is also a significant number of boys in the urban area who are street vendors and shop assistants. Girls in the urban sector are mainly domestic servants, baby sitters and shop assistants. Classifying by segment of activity, the largest percentage of children work in agriculture, followed by services, commerce, manufacturing and construction. The relatively poor Northeastern region has the highest percentage of working children, followed by the Southern region, where the number of agricultural households is very high. The smallest percentage of working children is observed in the Southeastern region, which is the richest in Brazil. As the sample does not include the rural areas of Rondônia, Acre, Amazonas, Roraima, Pará and Amapá State, in the Northern region, it therefore underestimates the percentage of working children. The States of Maranhão, Piauí, Ceará, Bahia, Paraíba e Pernambuco have the highest percentage of working children in Brazil.

As established in the framework, three sources of costs were obtained – the cost of providing a quality education to all children in lieu of work, the cost of programme interventions to alter attitudes and practices, and the opportunity cost of eliminating this work, i.e. the value of children's labour. On the benefit side, economic gains were calculated from a more educated population and a healthier population, since both more widespread education and the elimination of hazardous or unsuitable work have prospective health benefits.

The costs of the supply side of education were computed, involving school quality as well as quantity. The costs of achieving universal primary and lower secondary education encompass the additional costs of achieving net attendance rates (NAR) equal to 100%, which is the number of children out of school times the expenditure per pupil. Expenditures to improve school quality are those required to decrease the student-to-teacher ratio to an average of 40:1 and to finance purchases of material sufficient to reach the objective of 15% of overall recurrent education expenditures. Finally, capital expenditures include the cost of having enough school establishments to achieve the goal of universal coverage.

There were 1,208,542 children between 7 and 10 years old and 743,204 between 11 and 14 years old identified as out of school at the time of the survey. Children in pre-school or day care were also considered out of school.

The recurrent expenditure per student per year was estimated as \$441.06 PPP per student, based on data from the National Treasury Bureau, the Finance Ministry and the Ministry of Education. Those expenditures come from a Government National Fund to improve primary and secondary schools (FUNDEF), a State Quota of the Education Salary (QUESE), and a National Fund for Education Development (FNDE). Each state allocates 15% of four principal taxes (trade, export, state fund, county fund) to FUNDEF, and when a minimum amount per student is not reached (\$215 PPP in 1999), the federal government provides a supplement.

The pupil-teacher ratio was always below the required level of 40 pupils per classroom; therefore calculations to obtain the additional cost of achieving it were not necessary.

The amount of money coming from programmes other than FUNDEF, and therefore not used to pay teachers, relative to total recurrent expenditure, was very close to 15% in Brazil (14.6%). There were 20 states, out of 26, with a current non-wage expenditure of less than 15% of overall recurrent expenditure, and the calculation of additional costs was restricted to those states.

The gross enrolment rate (GER) provides an indication of the capacity of each level of the educational system, but a high ratio does not necessarily indicate a successful educational system as this ratio includes over-age and under-age enrolments. It can be assumed that when GER is above 100 there are enough school establishments for achieving the goal of universal coverage. In Brazil, the percentages failed to exceed 100% only for the 11 to 14-year-old children living in rural areas, with the exception of São Paulo and the Federal District.

Information on the amount the government spent specifically on school buildings is not available. The total amount spent on the QUESE programme was used as an approximation, since the money coming from this fund allows the construction of school buildings, the establishments' maintenance, and the purchase of consumption materials, among others. The costs for the supply side of education are presented in Table A4a.1.

In addition to this, we are assuming that there are three overriding factors that determine whether parents will choose to transfer their children from work to full time school attendance. First, education of sufficient quality must be readily available to them, which is the supply side of education. Second, they must be able to overcome the purely economic barriers to having their children engaged in study. This includes the direct cost of schooling, such as books and uniforms, but also, and especially, the opportunity cost – the value of the work children might have to give up if they increase their school participation. The third factor concerns populations requiring targeted intervention, which will be considered shortly.

Using the national household survey, children's monthly earnings, including salaries and payment in-kind, were used to determine the value of their work. The average monthly earnings were calculated for occupations related to domestic work, i.e., baby sitter, cleaner, cooker, cloth washer and so on. Since there was no information on hours spent in household activities, when a child was identified as performing domestic work and was not studying, we attributed to him or her a "domestic servant" salary derived from employed children. The earnings obtained in these ways were then combined to calculate an average opportunity cost for removing children from work.

To obtain the total opportunity cost of child labour, the number of working children from 5 to 14 years old, which was more than 3 million, was multiplied by the average opportunity cost. The results are presented in Table A4a.1.

A hypothetical income transfer that replaces 80% of the opportunity cost of children's work for all poor households was modeled in this study. Households with per capita income equal or below half the minimum salary per month (68 Reais or US$ 54.40 PPP) were classified as poor. This poverty line is the same as the one used by the *Bolsa Escola* programme. Household income was calculated from salaries, earnings in-kind, rents, retirements, pensions, interests from savings, and similar sources as they accrued to all members of the household, except from household employees, employees' relatives, renters and children below the age of 14. There were more than five and a half million households with one or more children 7 to 14 years of age below this poverty line in Brazil, encompassing nearly 12 million school-age children.

To obtain the costs of the income transfer programme, 80% of the opportunity cost of children's work was multiplied by the total number of children 7 to 14 years old from households at or below poverty line. The corresponding resource cost is then 5% of this amount (see Table A4a.1).

Finally, the intervention cost associated with the elimination of all of the worst forms of child labour was obtained multiplying the total number of individuals below 18 engaged in hazardous activities, which is 2,740,502, by the yearly expenditure per child with the PETI programme, i.e., $441.52 PPP. This almost certainly represents an overestimate, since a large percentage of this hazardous work would disappear in the course of implementing the rest of the model. On the other hand, there is an undetermined number of children working in unconditional worst forms and excluded from the hazardous count, and we would anticipate that most or all of them would require targeted interventions. On balance, it is likely that the first error (overestimation) exceeds the second.

For calculating the direct monetary benefits of increased education, the total number of children out of school (1,951,746) was multiplied by the number of years each child would need to complete eight years of education times the Mincerian coefficient (0.11) times the average unskilled adult's wage. This wage was obtained by averaging the earnings of all individuals from 20 to 60 years old with 1 year of education ($110.54/month), which is the average number of years of education for the children out of school. The present value of the total benefit was then obtained assuming that each person would receive earnings during 40 years of his or her life.

As shown in Table A4a.1, at a 5% interest rate, the benefits outweigh the costs by approximately a factor of 10.

The strength of this result in Brazil compared to the regional and global averages reported in the main body of the study can be attributed to two factors in particular. First, there is a higher ratio of the unskilled adult-to-child wage in Brazil. This leads to a greater discrepancy between the benefits of education on the one hand, and the opportunity and transfer costs on the other. Second, there is little capital cost entailed in expanding education. Even if the capital costs were to equal the recurrent, however, the enormous disparity between benefits and costs would not be in question.

Table A4a.1. Costs and benefits of eliminating child labour in Brazil, $million PPP

Wave	2001 to 2005	2006 to 2010	2011 to 2015	2016 to 2020	Total
Total costs	1 226	2 825	3 559	6 010	13 620
Education supply	211	1 285	2 413	4 101	8 010
Recurrent costs	187	1 219	2 334	4 070	7 811
Adjustments	24	57	72	26	180
Capital costs	–	8	6	5	19
Transfer implementation	75	124	64	174	437
Interventions	519	740	–	–	1 259
Opportunity cost	422	676	1 088	1 735	3 915
Total benefits	2 122	16 613	35 594	76 779	131 108
Education	2 040	16 408	35 317	76 503	130 268
Health	83	204	277	277	840
Net economic benefits	**896**	**13 788**	**32 035**	**70 769**	**117 487**
Transfer payments	1 497	2 481	1 271	3 489	8 737
Net financial benefits	**-601**	**11 307**	**30 764**	**67 280**	**108 750**

Annex 4b
COSTS AND BENEFITS
OF ELIMINATING CHILD LABOUR IN NEPAL

Children's work in Nepal is regulated under the Child Labour Prohibition and Regulation Act of 1999, according to which it is forbidden for any establishment to employ children under the age of 14. Nevertheless, child labour is common in this country, whose population is weighted toward youth. In particular, many children labour under conditions prohibited under ILO Convention 182 on the worst forms of child labour.

Of the total population of children ages 5 to 14, nearly 2.6 million, or 41.6%, have been identified as working, and just under 1.7 million, 26.7% of the total, have been deemed economically active. A narrower but still quite substantial category is occupied by the 1 million children who work but do not attend school. Most working children do not receive monetary compensation, although 6% do.

By far the most common activity in which working children are found is agriculture, accounting for nearly 95% of the total. Girls make up the majority of all these workers, and they are less likely to receive education than boys. Of those children receiving money wages, it is common for parents to collect and keep them.

Because of the commitment of Nepal's government and several NGOs, there has recently been a series of studies documenting the child labour problem. Detailed data were collected in the National Child Labour Survey of 1996 (Suwal et al., 1997), and subsequent reports published by the National Planning Commission and the Ministry of Labour provide additional information. Also, ILO-IPEC has conducted five Rapid Assessments, focusing on child porters, rag pickers, domestic workers, bonded labour and child trafficking. Unfortunately, different studies often disagree in their findings, and there has been no effort to consolidate them.

For the purposes of this study, these sources provided primary inputs, but were supplemented by several others. Most important were the National Living Standard Survey (NLSS) of 1996 and the Nepal Labour Force Survey (NLFS) of 1999. The NLSS was a household survey undertaken with technical support from the World Bank. The sample size was 3,775 households, and the survey instrument yielded data on the number and characteristics of poor households, adult and child wage rates, and population weights used to adjust data from other sources. The NLFS was administered with financial support from UNDP and technical assistance from the ILO. It provided the micro-data used in this study to estimate a Mincerian coefficient. It also provided the basis for estimates of the extent and distribution of child labour. In addition to these, a further significant resource was the 20-Year Education Projection Model prepared for the World Bank Education Sector Review. This was the basis for estimates of net enrolment rates in primary and lower secondary education.

The largest cost of implementing the hypothetical child labour elimination model in Nepal is that of providing for expanded education quantity and quality. In all subsequent discussions of education it should be borne in mind that Nepal's age categories for primary and lower secondary school do not correspond to those employed in the global report. For purposes of consistency, it was necessary to standardize on a single set of age groupings, even though each country has its own framework. For the global report, this meant that ages 6 to 11 were assigned to primary schools and 12 to 14 to secondary. In the case of Nepal, however, the corresponding brackets are 6 to 10 and 11 to 13. In this annex, freed from the necessity of conforming to an international standard, we adopt the local framework. This indicates, however, that the economic totals relating to education would require adjustment in order to be compared to the regional and total amounts reported in the main body of the study.

Net attendance at the primary level is 57%; at the lower secondary level it is only 19%. There are substantial differences in these rates across regions within Nepal, but only national averages will be employed here. Among primary school age children, socially disadvantaged groups, and particularly the girls among them, are over-represented among those not in attendance.

Evidently, a significant expansion of education is envisioned. The current pupil-teacher ratio is 38 in primary and 37 in lower secondary, taken at a national average. Assuming the ability to shift teachers from areas of low to high PTR, no additional adjustment is required beyond that needed to accommodate the increased number of students. Although poor in quality, the number of school facilities at the primary level is sufficient at present to accommodate full attendance by 2015. Approximately 9,000 new lower secondary schools will need to be built, however. The costs of additional teachers, non-personnel expenditures and new capital facilities were calculated from a variety of education reports. It is interesting to note that the unit capital cost was two and a half times as large as the unit recurrent cost at the primary level, but only 40% larger at the lower secondary.

A second principal cost of eliminating child labour derives from the contributions these children make to household income. Survey data on paid child labour was extrapolated to unpaid labour based on work of a similar type. Since only daily compensation was reported, it was assumed that an average child's work year consists of 100 days; this resulted in the annual estimate of $343 PPP. To defray households for the loss of this contribution, an income transfer programme was modelled. (Such a programme would also defray the costs imposed on parents for sending their children to school, which can be substantial in Nepal.) Setting the poverty line at $376 PPP (based on World Bank subsistence estimates), it was found that just over 1.25 million families with school age children can be classified as poor, and their average poverty gap is $160 PPP. With a high number of such children per family and a high ratio of the working child's productivity to the poverty line, our formula for unit transfers was not sensitive at all to estimates of the poverty gap, however.

A final component of cost is the need for programmes to target particular groups, either those for whom the income transfer may not provide a sufficient basis for the elimination of child labour, or those whose involvement in worst forms suggests the need for other sorts of interventions. Into this first category fall the *dalit*, a socially excluded cast group. 76,555 children are targeted on this basis. Into the second fall children engaged in bonded and other worst forms of child labour, for which the available estimate is 129,126. The study does not incorporate the potential needs of the refugee population from Bhutan, approximately 100,000 in all. The unit cost of intervention was calculated from existing IPEC programmes operative in Nepal.

There are two sources of economic benefits anticipated in the model, the most important of which derives from increased education. The key elements in the formula for calculating this are the number of children to receive increased education (already discussed above), the Mincerian coefficient and the average unskilled adult wage. The Mincerian coefficient was calculated from household micro-data. It was found to be approximately 0.07, with the estimating equation having an adjusted R^2 of 0.35. Note that this is significantly less than the baseline coefficient of 0.11 used in the global report; it presumably reflects differences in the Nepalese economy's utilization of human capital. The adult wage was derived from the surveys mention above.

The economic benefit of improved health was calculated for Nepal in the same way as for other countries: survey data provided the distribution of child workers across sectors, and this composition was used in conjunction with the Fassa (2003) study to estimate disability-adjusted life years (DALYs). These in turn were converted to monetary estimates based on comparison with other health stressors and Nepal's income per capita.

Table A4b.1 summarizes the present value calculation of the costs and benefits at a 5% discount rate.

Table A4b.1. Total economic costs and benefits of eliminating child labour in Nepal, in $million PPP

Total cost	**6 118**
Opportunity cost	2 117
Transfer programme	126
Interventions	131
Education supply	3 744
Total benefits	**7 024**
Education	6 982
Health	42
Net economic benefits	**906**
Income transfers	2 529
Net financial benefits	**-1 623**

The net benefit in the case of Nepal is positive but smaller than those found at the regional and global levels, due to the high ratio of child-to-adult wages and the low estimate of the returns to education. Note that, at a Mincerian coefficient of 0.11 (as used in the global report), net financial benefits would be positive as well. In any event, it should be remembered that transfer costs are not resource costs in the economic sense; hence the positive outcome of the exercise remains intact.

A second way to consider the impact of the elimination model is as a sequence of net annual flows, as described in Chapter 9 of the global report. Table A4b.2 presents these data for Nepal.

Table A4b.2. Annual flows of net costs of eliminating child labour in Nepal, in $million PPP

Year	Net Flow
1	-109
2	-134
3	-160
4	-187
5	-214
6	-308
7	-340
8	-373
9	-408
10	-444
11	-482
12	-526
13	-575
14	-630
15	-692
16	-656
17	-671
18	-683
19	-694
20	-703

As can be seen, these flows, on an undiscounted basis, become increasingly negative throughout the 20-year period. Of course, given the results in Table A4b.1 (which incorporate the effect of discounting), extension into subsequent years would show much larger and fully offsetting positive net flows. Table A4b.3 presents the same information, but also including the income transfers (which are not economic costs).

Table A4b.3. Annual flows of the financial costs of eliminating child labour in Nepal, in $million PPP

Year	Net Flow
1	-150
2	-216
3	-283
4	-351
5	-420
6	-554
7	-627
8	-702
9	-778
10	-855
11	-934
12	-1 020
13	-1 110
14	-1 205
15	-1 308
16	-1 314
17	-1 369
18	-1 423
19	-1 475
20	-1 525

Clearly the financial burden of implementing the programme exceeds its resource cost. At the end of the 20-year horizon, the model anticipates a funding requirement of $1.5 billion PPP.

Annex 4c
COSTS AND BENEFITS
OF ELIMINATING CHILD LABOUR IN KENYA

Kenya provides an example of a country with significant child labour and shortfalls in school attendance that is well positioned to benefit from a vigorous child labour elimination programme. This is a young country; more than half the population is below the age of 18, and a quarter are of school age as defined in this study, ages 6 to 14. It is relatively poor, with a per capita income of $1,010 in 2000. Due to unfavourable macroeconomic conditions, particularly external debt (and an associated structural adjustment programme), Kenya's economic development has stalled, and education statistics even show a decline during the 1990s. Nevertheless, as we shall see, the returns are lower than we might expect due to factors that increase the costs and reduce the benefits.

Overall results for the economic costs and benefits of eliminating child labour in Kenya are provided in Table A4c.1.

Table A4c.1. Total economic costs and benefits of eliminating child labour in Kenya, in $million PPP

Total cost	**4 715**
Opportunity cost	224
Transfer programme	14
Interventions	100
Education	4 377
Total benefits	**5 788**
Education	5 677
Health	111
Net economic benefits	**1 073**
Transfer payments	277
Net financial benefits	**796**

Both net economic and net financial benefits are comfortably positive, but the ratio is not as great as we saw in the global study. The internal rate of return, 6.3%, is also lower. The reasons will become clear as we examine the individual cost and benefit items.

Education supply. Before proceeding to the actual calculations, it should be noted that Kenya's educational system is organized on the basis of eight years of primary school, covering ages 6 to 14, and four years of secondary after that. We chose, however, to evaluate changes in the educational system as if Kenya had the "standard" system of primary education through age 11 and lower secondary through age 14. We did this to facilitate comparisons between Kenya's results and those described for other countries and regions.

The public expenditure on recurrent costs per pupil at the primary level was $158 in 2000 PPP; to this must be added an additional $30 in direct household costs. But non-personnel costs made up only 2.8% of all such recurrent expenses in 2000, requiring an additional adjustment of $27. As we have already seen (Chapter 4), the HIV/AIDS epidemic will impose even more costs on the system; we calculated this to be a further $13 per student. Thus the combined unit cost comes to $228.

The Kenya study team was unable to locate reliable information on the costs of school construction. Based on discussions with education officials, they made a rough estimate of $14,886 as the cost per primary classroom, including desks and other non-building items; at 30 students per room this yielded a unit capital cost of $496.

The net attendance rate in Kenya at the primary level was determined to be 88.3% based on household survey data. Given the population of Kenyans ages 6 to 11 and a projected growth rate for this group of 1.2% per year, we arrived at the totals contained in Table A4c.2.

Secondary costs were calculated in much the same manner. Public recurrent expenses per pupil were $530 and households contributed an additional $409. Since non-personnel expenditures made up only 5.5% of the total, an additional adjustment of $105 was required. After a further adjustment for the effects of HIV/AIDS, the unit recurrent cost became $1,110 – substantially more than the amount at the primary level. We noted, however, that these expenses really apply only to 14 year-olds, one third of the age group we identify in this study as lower secondary. Hence we applied only one-third of the recurrent cost difference to lower secondary students as a whole, producing a revised unit cost of $522. The country team also estimated the cost of constructing a new classroom; divided by the number of students per room, this came to a unit capital cost of $532. The same adjustment for distinguishing between 14 year-olds and those aged 12 to 14 was made, resulting in a revised unit capital cost of $508. Taking account of the low NAR for this group of 23%, initial population size and a projected annual population growth rate of 0.8%, we generated the costs found in Table A4c.2.

As this table clearly demonstrates, the costs of expanding and upgrading education in Kenya are dominated by those at the lower secondary level, despite the much larger number of children in the primary age group. This is due mainly to the great disparity in net attendance rates and, to a lesser extent, to the differences in unit costs.

Table A4c.2. Costs of education supply in Kenya, in $million PPP

Level	Wave 1	Wave 2	Wave 3	Wave 4	Total
Primary	154	204	274	367	1 000
Secondary		657	1 000	1 749	3 407
Total	**154**	**861**	**1 274**	**2 117**	**4 407**

Transfer programme. From household surveys, it is estimated that there are over 2.6 million families with school-age children living in poverty in Kenya, and that these families average 2.2 children each. Using our formula for income transfers based on the value of child labour (see below) and the average poverty gap of $169, the average transfer per family is $58. The reason it falls so far below the poverty gap is that the value of child labour ($33) is itself a small fraction of this gap. Over a twenty-year period in which additional families are progressively encompassed within the system, and discounting to the year 2000, the overall amount of income transferred is $276.9 million. Above this, 5% or $13.8 million are earmarked for administering the programme.

Interventions. It was difficult to perform this calculation, given the paucity of data concerning socially excluded children and children in the worst forms of child labour. There are certainly many children engaged in unconditional worst forms, but there have been no formal enumerations of them. To identify children in hazardous occupations, the Kenyan researchers classified nine such occupations and determined, from household surveys, that approximately 760,000 children were engaged in them. From UNHCR, an additional 90,000 children were recorded as socially excluded. From our survey of IPEC programmes, we found that the unit cost of interventions in Kenya was $240. Anticipating the implementation of programmes to address the needs of 850,000 children over a ten-year period, and incorporating discounting, we arrived at a present value cost of just over $100 million.

Opportunity costs. Of the more than 8.6 million children between the ages of 5-14 in Kenya, just under 2 million are classified as engaged in child labour. To determine the cost to households and the economy in general of withdrawing their labour, we needed to attach a value to this work. A SIMPOC survey administered in 1998-99 found that the average earnings of a child worker in Kenya were $32.58. Thus, we arrived at our calculation of the opportunity cost:

$$1\,993\,584 \text{ children} \times \$32.58 \text{ per child} \times 20 \text{ years} = \$1\,299\,019\,026$$

Note, however, that this labour is not all removed immediately. Our programme calls for its progressive elimination over a ten-year period. Hence the figure will be reduced, because of fewer child-years eliminated and discounting, to $223,889,669.

Education benefits. In the absence of direct household survey measurement, we imputed an average unskilled wage of $405, not unreasonable in light of the country's per capita income of $1,010. We also utilized the standard Mincerian coefficient of 0.11, meaning that each additional year of education was expected to increase an individual's earnings by 11%. One important difference between Kenya and other countries, however, is that in Kenya the average work expectancy is only 30 years, rather than the 40 we employed throughout this study. We chose, nevertheless, to use 40 years as the basis for our baseline estimate of economic benefits. The main reason for this is that the 30-year figure is backward-looking, and it is reasonable to expect that with economic and social improvements, Kenyans' work profiles will begin to resemble those in better-off countries. On the other hand, of course, the prevalence of HIV/AIDS casts a shadow over the future, even though current indications are that this prevalence has begun to slowly recede. It is worth noting that the difference between 30 and 40 years of education benefits is not as large as might be expected, due to the effect of discounting. Our baseline (40-year) estimate is $5,677 million, and reducing this to 30 years results in $5,086 – not enough to reverse the conclusion that overall net economic (and financial) benefits are positive.

Health benefits. Based on the detailed occupational classifications utilized in the Kenya SIMPOC survey, we were able to apply our DALY formula (Chapter 8) and arrive at an estimate of 38,700 DALYs attributable to hazardous employment of children. As we pointed out in that chapter, this should be regarded as an underestimate of the true health cost, perhaps a large underestimate. Our baseline relationship between DALYs and percentages of GNI per capita yields the result summarized in Table A4c.1.

Considering all of these items, it is apparent that, as in other countries and regions, the relationship between education costs and benefits has the largest impact on the amount of net benefits. The relatively small net economic benefits in this case are attributable primarily to the low unskilled wage in relation to the cost of educating a child. The unit recurrent cost of primary education, for instance, is $288, but the one-year benefit associated with this expense is only $45, i.e. 11% of $405, the relevant wage rate. The accumulation of many such benefit years, as the former child lives out his or her working life, guarantees that the overall net benefits will be positive, even with the addition of capital costs, but they are less so in Kenya than elsewhere.

The annual undiscounted net financial flows for the first 20 years are given in Figure A4c.1. At their most negative point, in 2008, they represent 0.6% of Kenya's GNI for 2000.

A more precise measurement of the resource implications of administering our hypothetical programme in Kenya is given by the public sector costs, which we have defined as the sum of education supply costs, intervention costs and transfer costs (both the income transfers themselves and the administrative overhead) minus 20% of the concurrent economic benefits from health and education. Figure A4c.2 shows the trajectory over the twenty years of programme implementation.

Several patterns are noticeable. The fiscal burden takes a great leap in year 6 when secondary education expansion begins. It recedes in year 11, following the completion of the interventions targeting the worst forms. It finally begins to decline in year 17, as 20% of the increasing benefits begin

Figure A4c.1. Undiscounted net financial flows due to child labour elimination in Kenya, in $million PPP

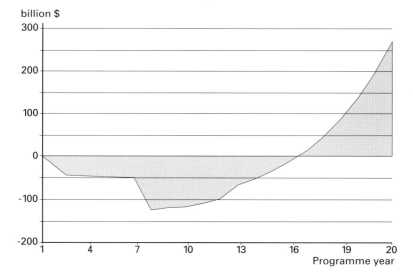

Figure A4c.2. Public sector costs of child labour elimination in Kenya, 2000-2020, in $million PPP

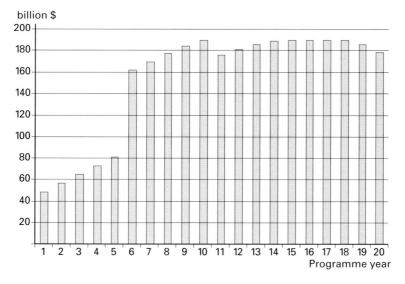

to outweigh the annual growth in transfer costs. The peak year is 2016, when the public sector cost is $192.4 million. This sum represents 0.66% of Kenya's GNI for 2000, a substantial but clearly affordable investment.